AuthorHouse™
1663 Liberty Drive
Bloomington, IN 47403
www.authorhouse.com
Phone: 1 (800) 839-8640

Published by AuthorHouse   06/18/2015

ISBN: 978-1-4918-4976-7 (sc)
ISBN: 978-1-4969-7319-1 (e)

Joseph Guillet

A Port-A-John
in
Iraq

Compiled by Erick and Joseph

Compiled by Erick and Joseph from anonymous photos and emails.

authorHOUSE®

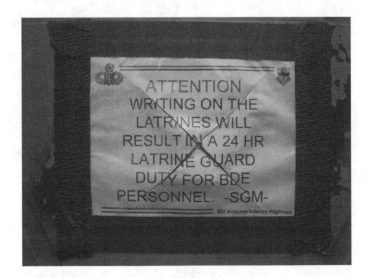

INTRODUCTION

"A PORT-A-JOHN IN IRAQ"

These pictures were collected during Operation Iraqi (OIF) 06-07 in different camps in Iraq. The military is hierarchical. The opinion of the soldiers, airmen, sailors and marines don't count. Basically, you do what you are told to do and accomplish the mission to its best. Therefore, the only way soldiers can express themselves freely is through graffiti inside a Port-a-John. Pictures were gathered through different camps. It is remarkable how the morale of these soldiers, airmen, sailors, and marines changes depending upon the location. At the same time, like everything in life, you find the two opposite sides of the coin: good and bad. It is amazing how some individuals despite temperatures of 100 degrees Fahrenheit will still manage to perpetuate their thoughts on the walls of the Port-a-John for others to admire.

The Port-a-John turns out to be a one-to-one open book of soldiers, sailors, airmen and marines feelings. Like an outlet of discouragement, pride, drive, hate, and in some cases, hope. For some, writing on these walls became an emotional relief, just knowing that someone will read them and share their burdens. The most common was "I hated my boss" kind of attitude. The United States Military is a big melting pot, with people from different parts of the nation and the world; yet hate, racism, and the condition to put others down were always there. Some Soldiers will open up to their sexuality. Others will make sure their hatred toward other ethnic groups are heard.

Like they say, "A picture is worth a thousand words" and the book, "A Port-a-John in Iraq" is just that, a compilation of pictures expressing the fighters thoughts until they get removed.

Maybe one of these Port-a-John artists is probably out of the military or still in the service. Hopefully he or she will recognize the art work and finally be satisfied that the arts are no longer anonymous but open to anyone to read and understand the drive behind them.

Try to go into a filthy Port-a-John in the desert with temperature of over 100 degrees Fahrenheit and still manage to concentrate, carry a permanent marker and write your thoughts for others to see.

Maybe you can find your art inside this book.

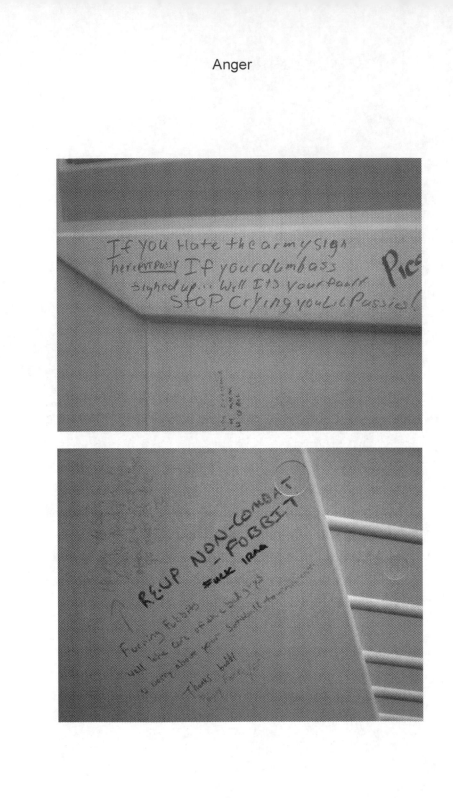

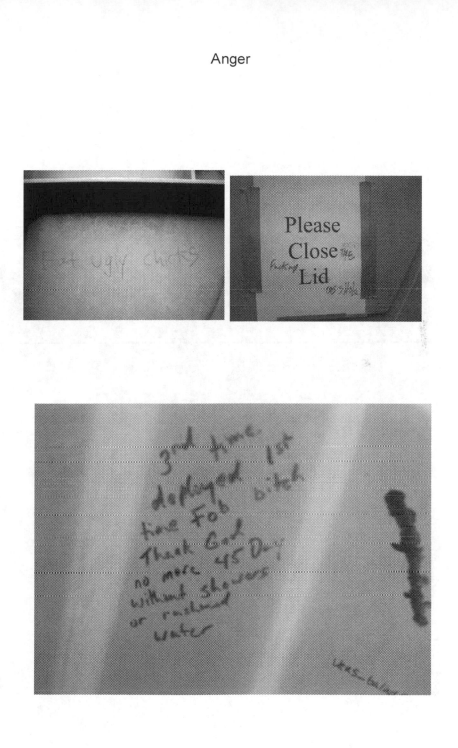

Anger

Sick Fucker
— I had a threesome w/ your mom & sister too! They're great!

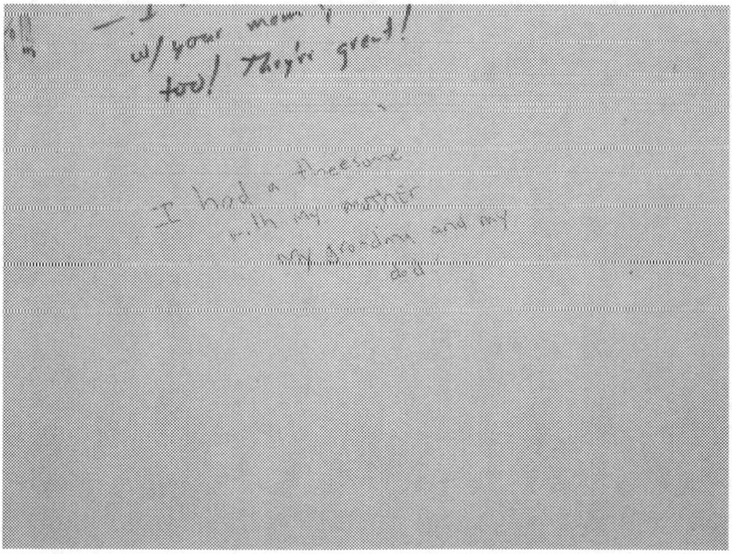

w/ your mom &
too! They're great!
I had a threesome
with my mother
my grandma and my
dad

Anger

It does
for us
who go
outside the
wife

SUCKZ
SO Does
your mom
But No One
Complaind

THIS PLACE

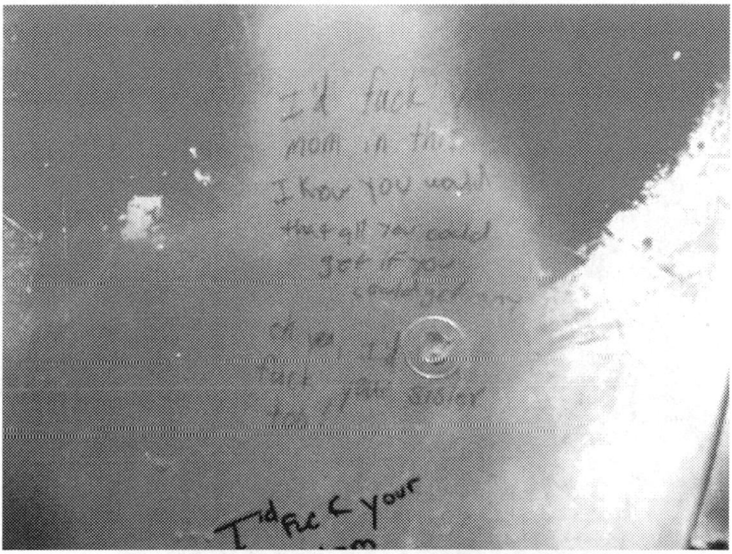
I'd fuck your

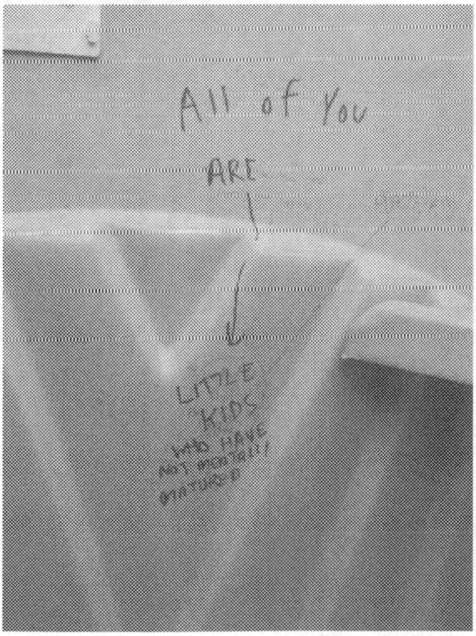
All of You
ARE
LITTLE
KIDS
WHO HAVE

Anger

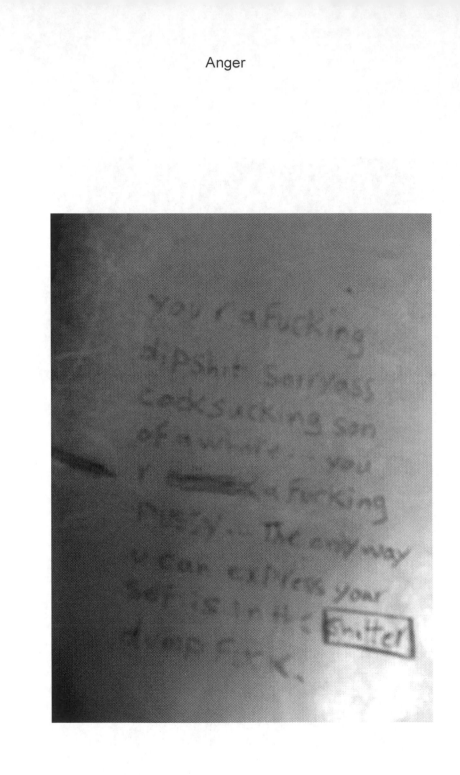

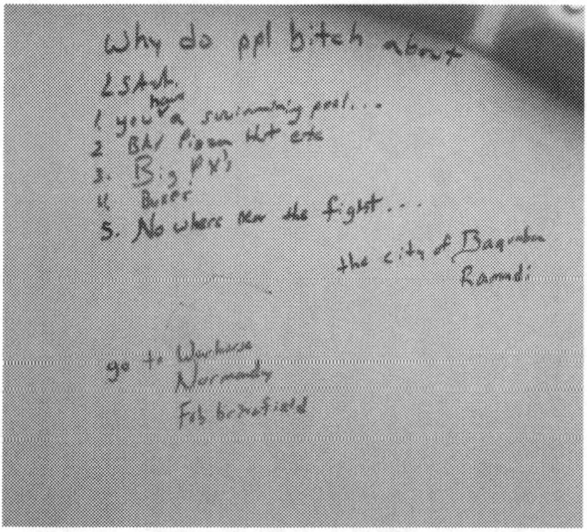
Why do ppl bitch about
LSAh.
1 you have a swimming pool...
2 BK/ Pizza Hut etc
3. Big PX's
4 Beer
5. No where near the fight...
the city of Baghdad
Ramadi
go to
Normandy
Fob

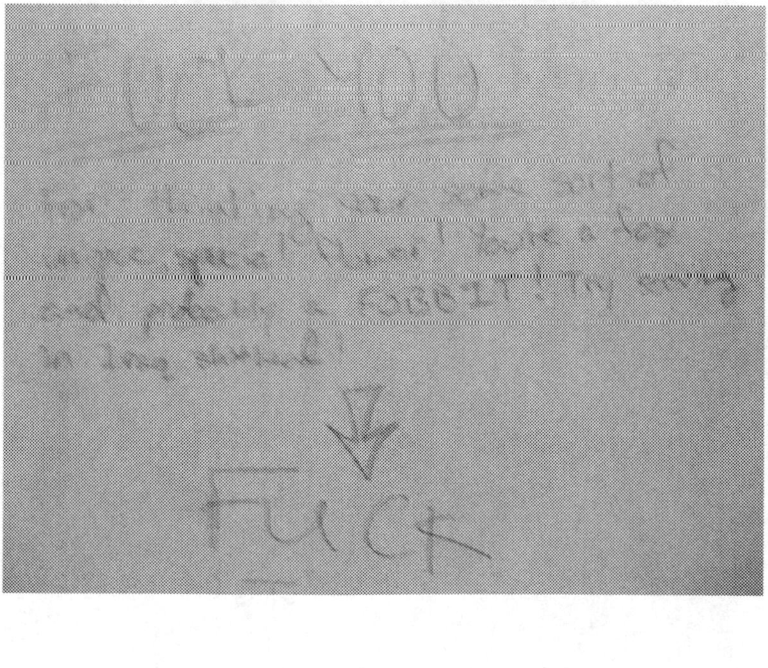
FUCK

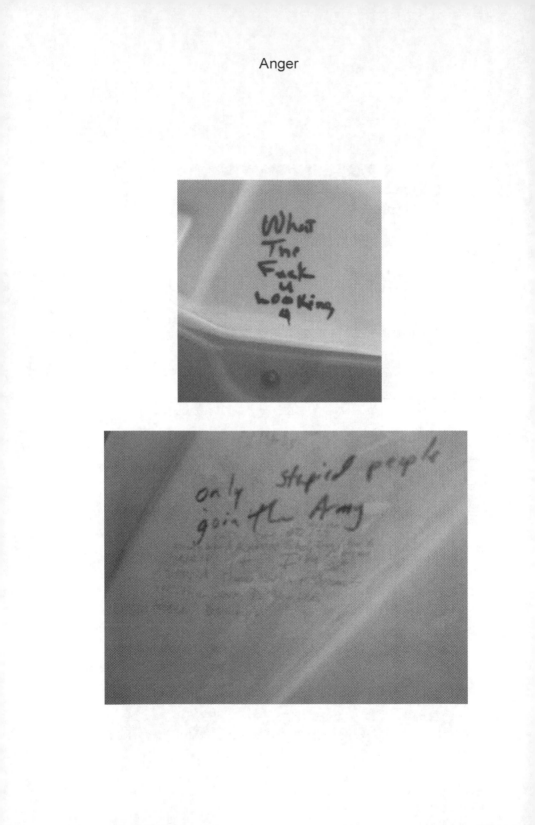

If it wasn't for
AIRPOWER you dumb
would bedead
Sorry our ASVAB scores
were to High Retards

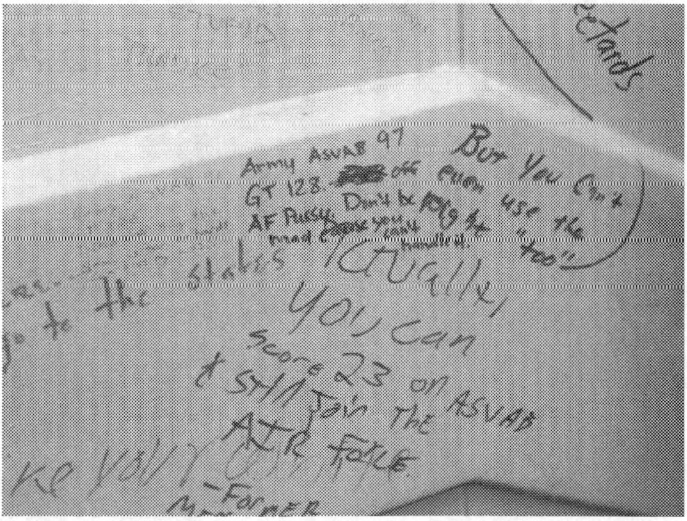
Army ASVAB 97
GT 128.
But You Can't use the "too"
you can
score 23 on ASVAB
& still Join the
AIR Force
-Former

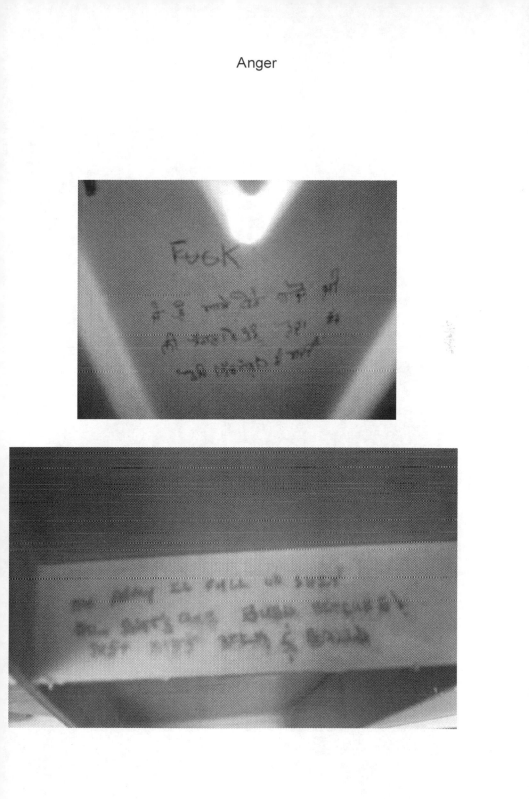

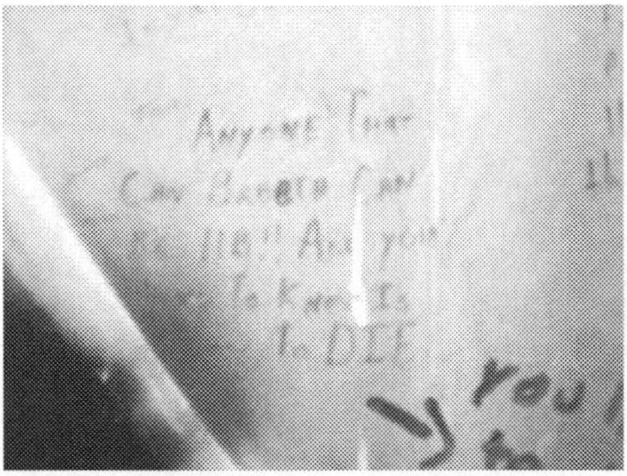

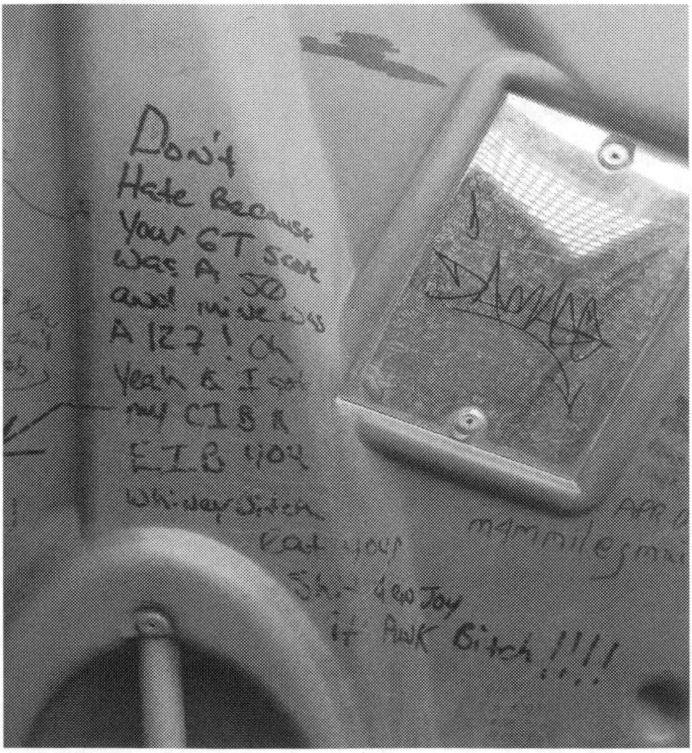
Don't
Hate Because
Your GT Score
Was A 50
and mine was
A 127! Oh
Yeah & I got
my CIB &
EIB you
Whiney bitch

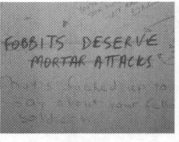

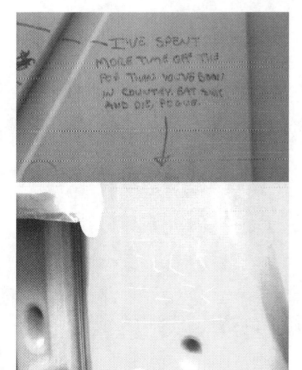

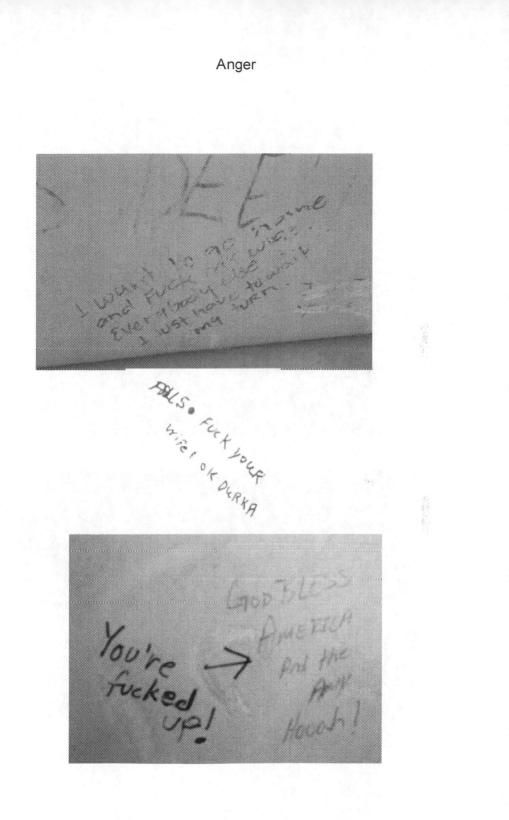

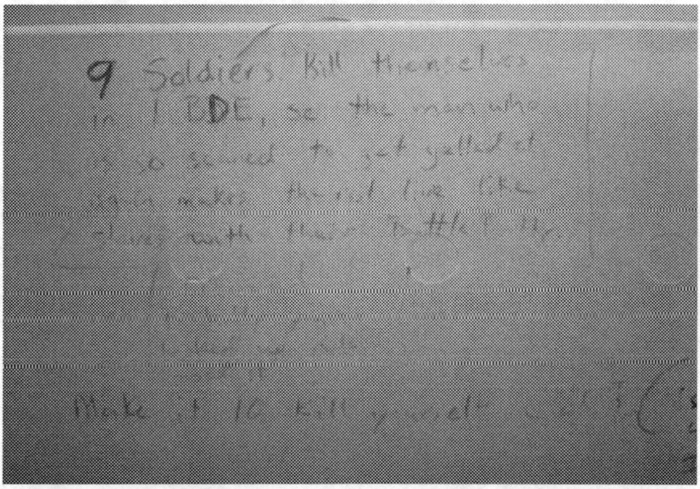
9 Soldiers kill themselves

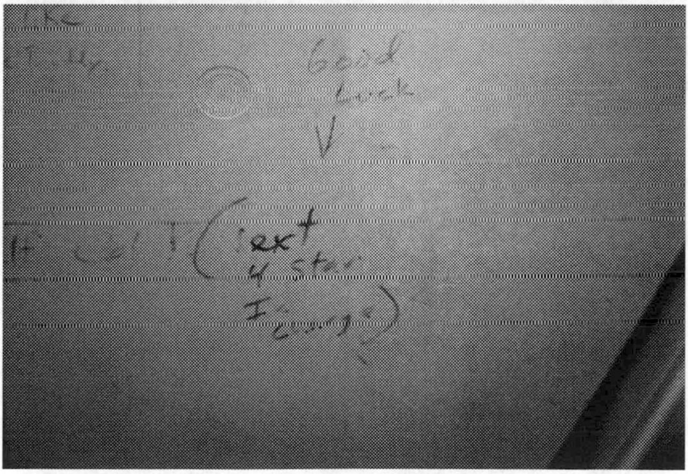
Good
luck

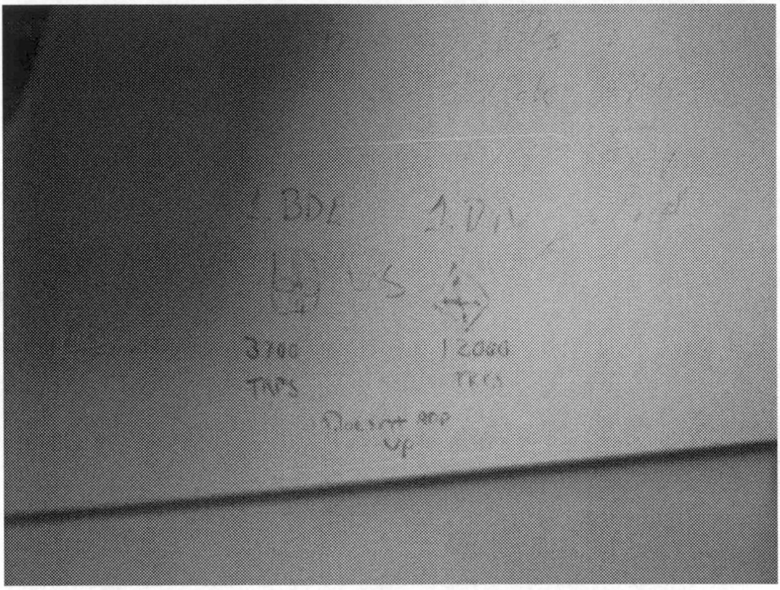
1. BDL
3700
TPS
12000

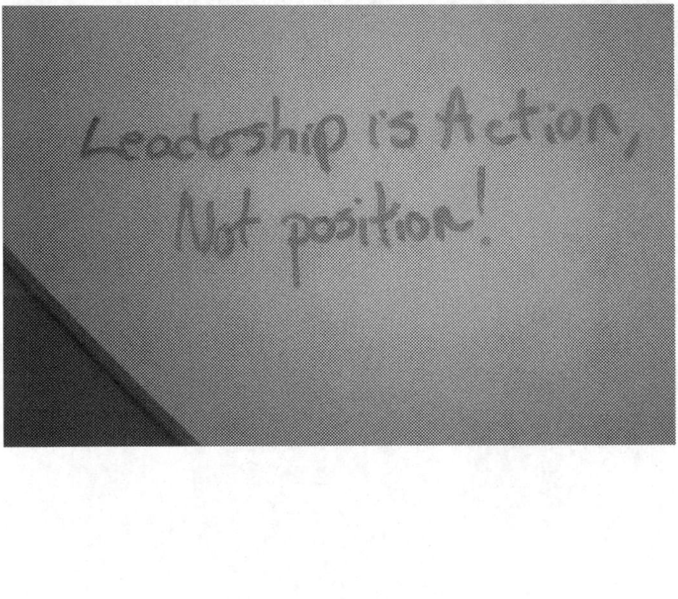
Leadership is Action,
Not position!

Inspiration

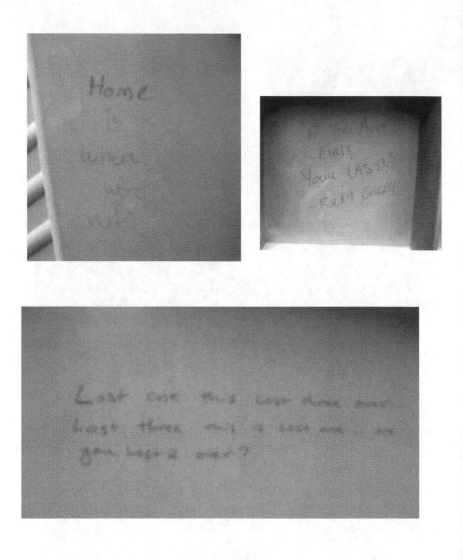

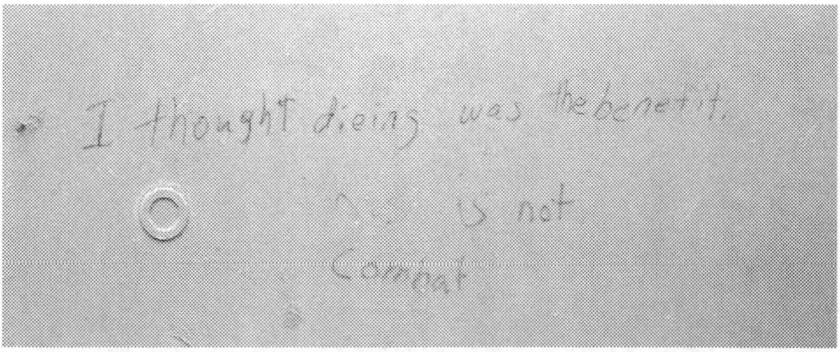
I thought dieing was the benefit.
is not

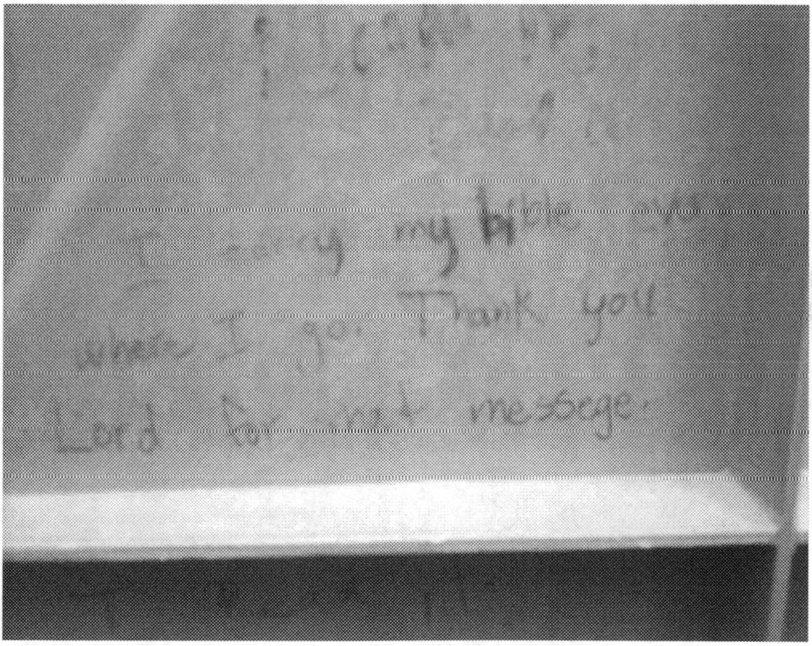
Thank you
message

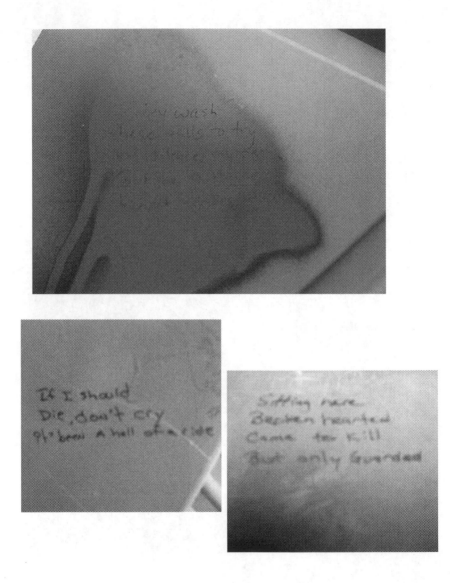

Inspiration

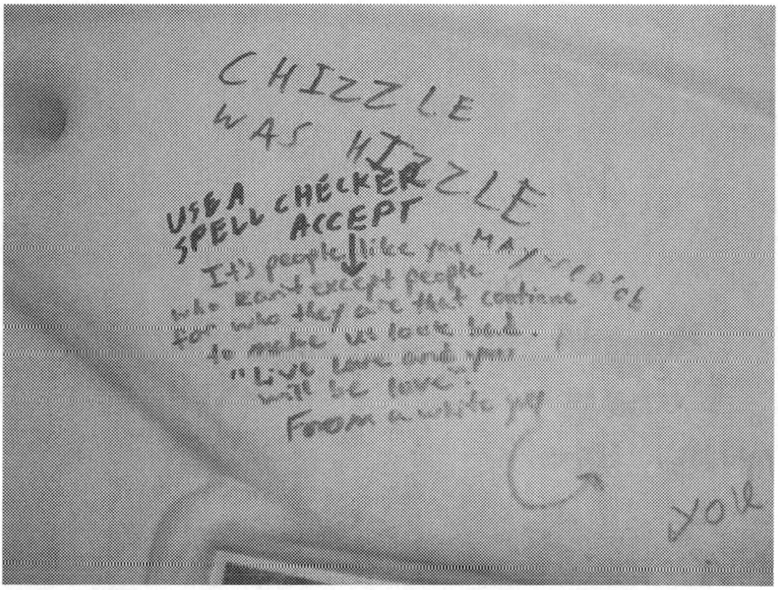

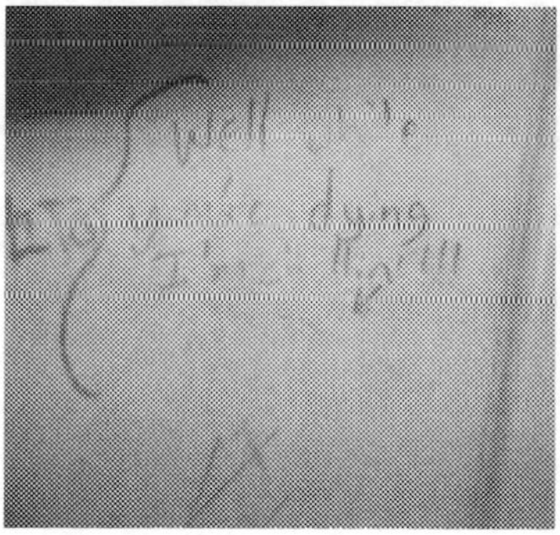

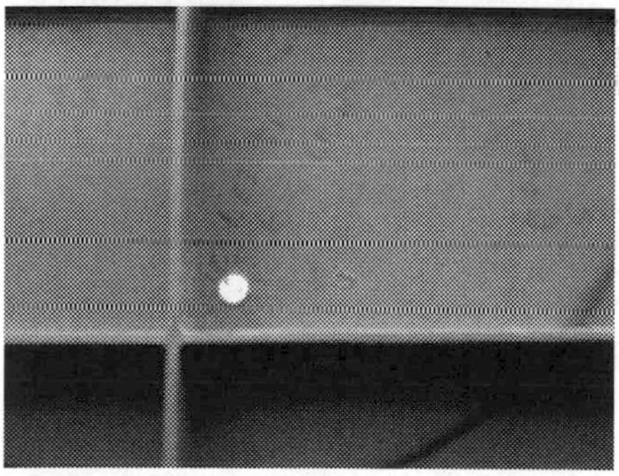

with kindness
repay the kind
friend.

But with lies
repay, the false
friend with lies.

We're
all
getting
screwed
by the
man!

Birdy Birdy
In the sky...
Why'd you do that,
In my eye?

You suck
Your Mom. Sucks more!
Nothing captures human interest, like human tragedy.
If I had one, I would!

Inspiration

Inspiration

Inspiration

FOBBITS DESERVE MORTAR ATTACKS

That's fucked up to say about your fellow soldiers.

Life is but a moment, just enjoy your roll!!!

EVERYONE IS ESSENTIAL IN THIS WAR. EVERYONE!! NO MATTER IF THEY GO OUTSIDE THE WIRE OR NOT. WE ALL NEED EACH OTHER.
(SPOKEN LIKE A TRUE SOLDIER)

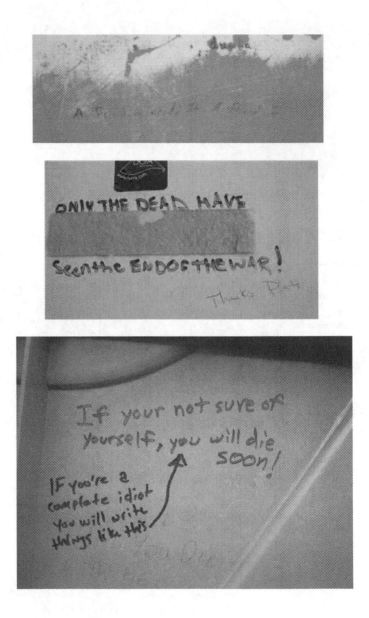

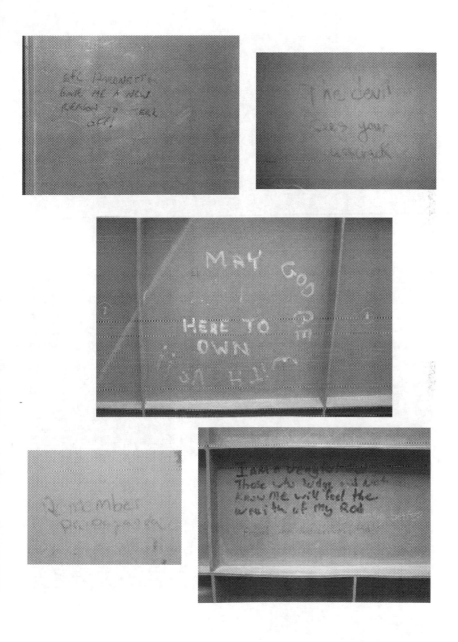

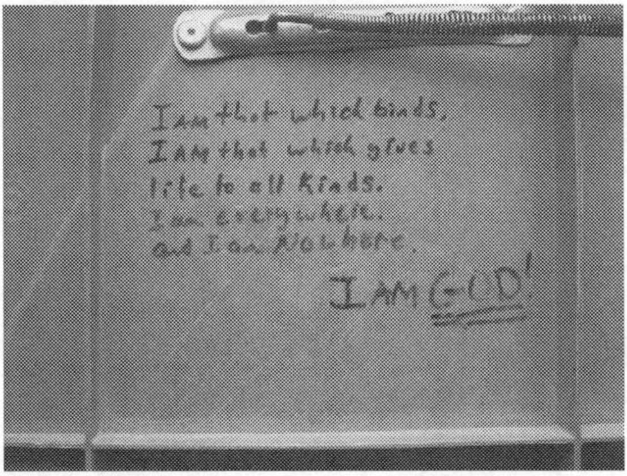
I am that which binds,
I AM that which gives
life to all kinds.
I am everywhere.
and I am Nowhere.
I AM GOD!

Have you ever seen
Tweetle beetles have a Paddle
battle.
Better yet Tweetle beetles have a Paddle
Battle in a Puddle
Or even Better a tweetle beetle
Pudde Paddle battle in a bottle.
Now that's good fun.
—Fox 'n' Socks.
- I.R.A.

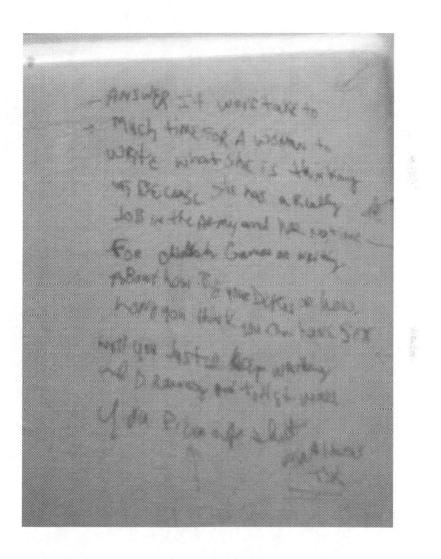

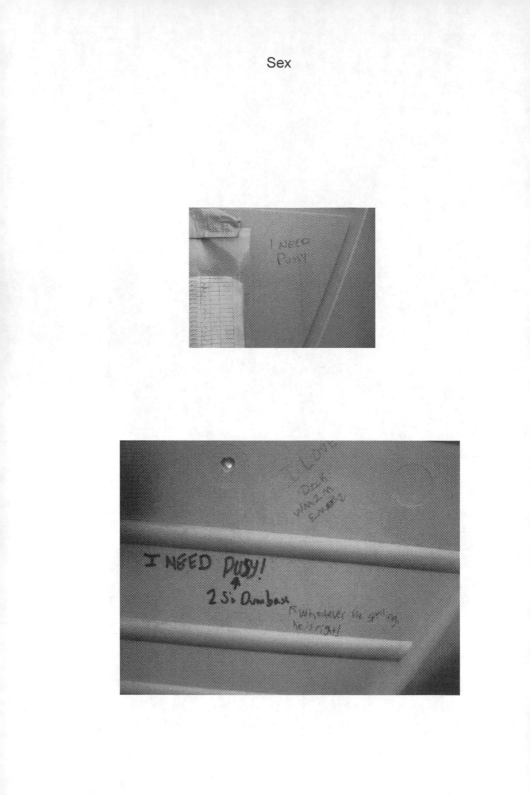

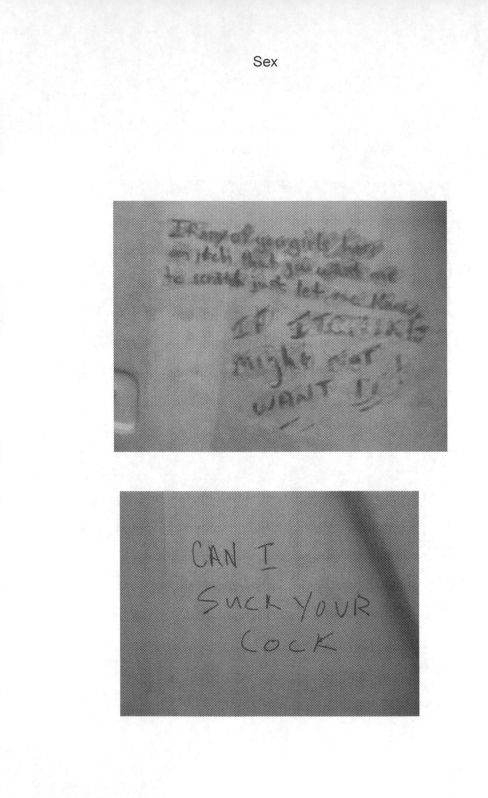

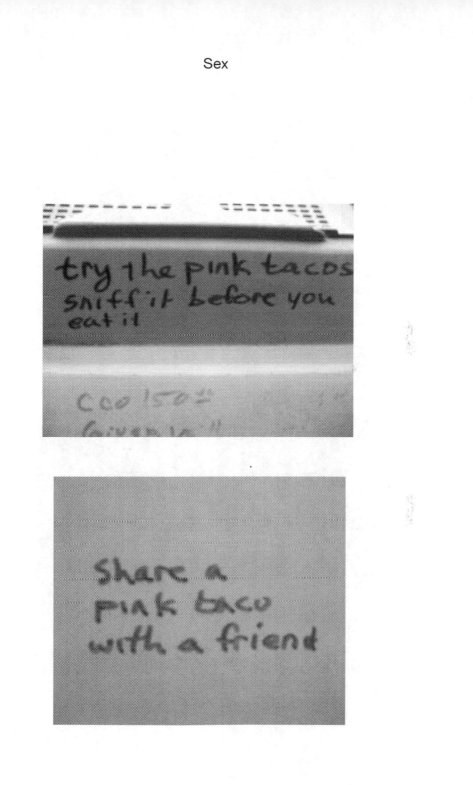

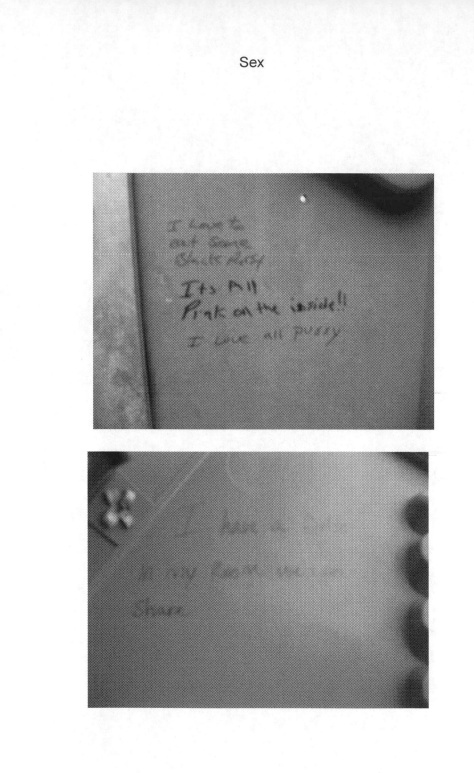

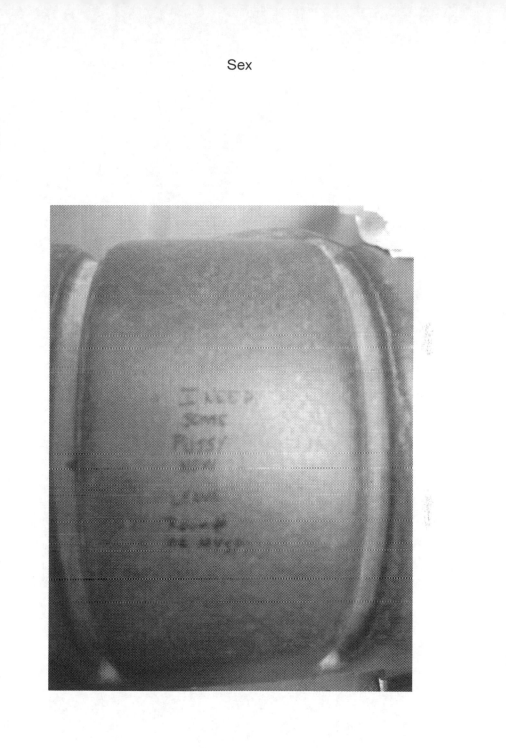

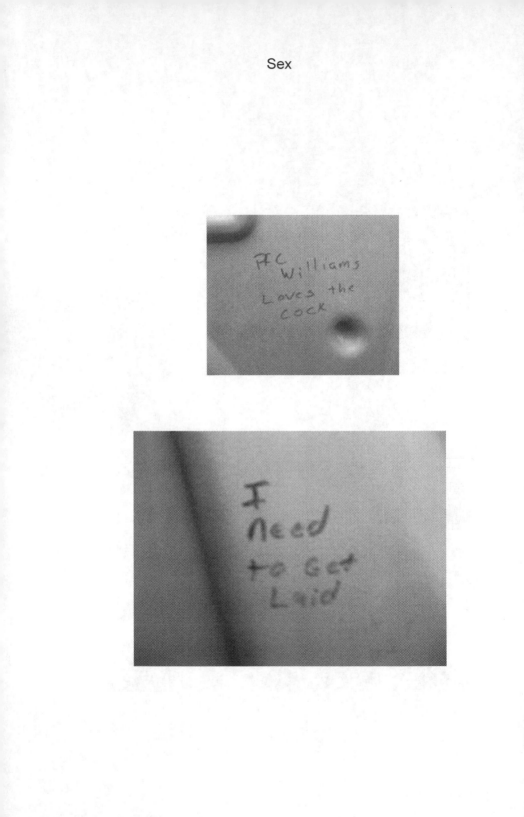

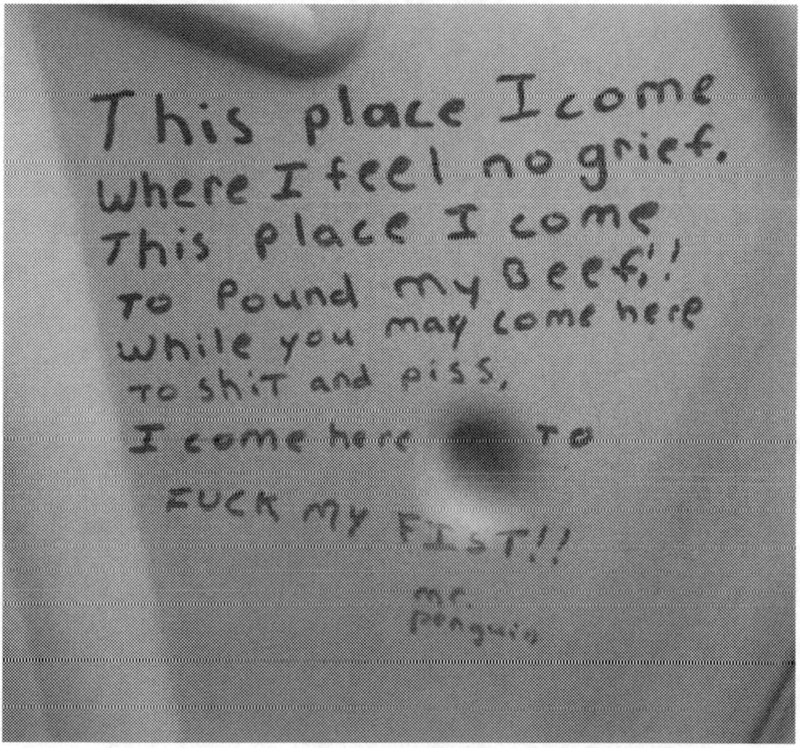
This place I come
Where I feel no grief.
This place I come
To Pound my Beef!!
While you may come here
To shit and piss,
I come here to
FUCK my FIST!!
Mr.
Penguin

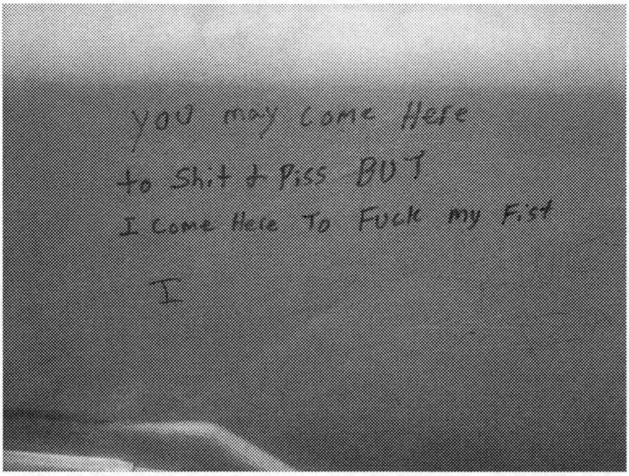
you may come Here
to Shit & Piss BUT
I come Here To Fuck my Fist
I

Don't DO
IT
DADDY
OIF 06.08
myspace.com/kristhou

Sex

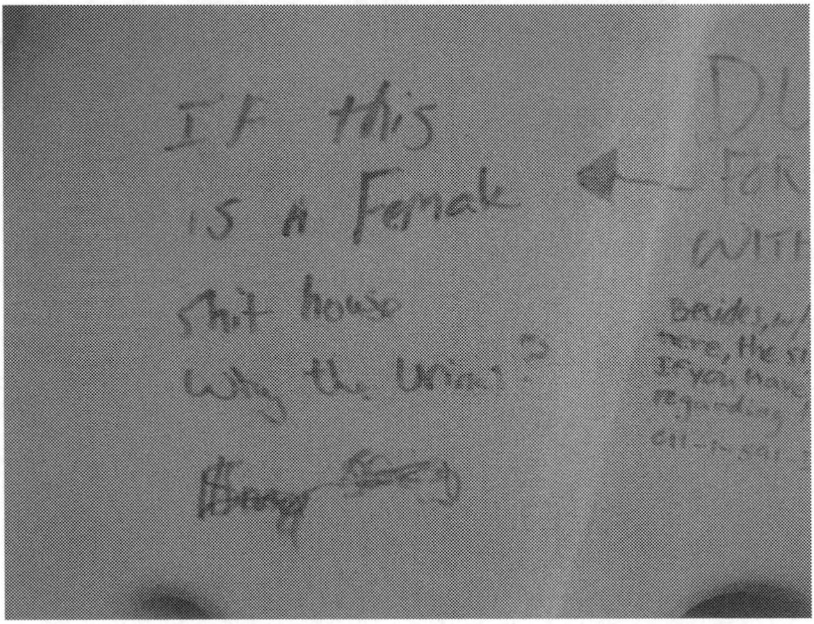
IF this
is a Female
shit house
why the Urinal ?

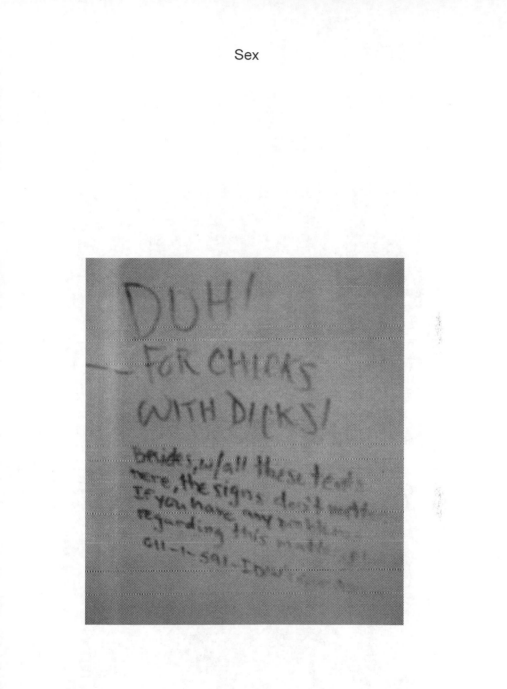

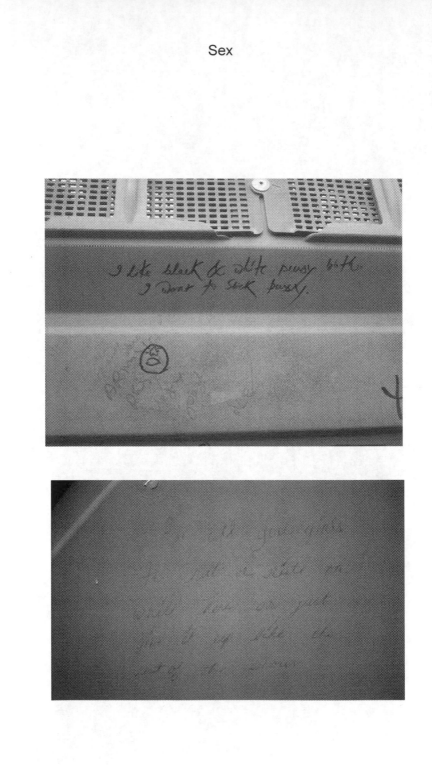

Any Females
wanna Fuck come to
H-7 J-25

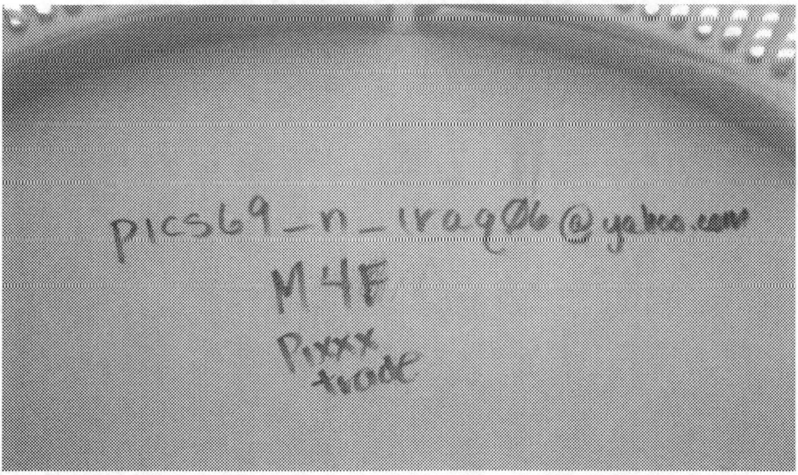
pics69_n_iraq06@yahoo.com
M4F
Pixxx
trade

Ugandan Dont act like u are an
american Soldier, you're not you are
a fucking guard only at Dfac.
thanx
Fuck u all

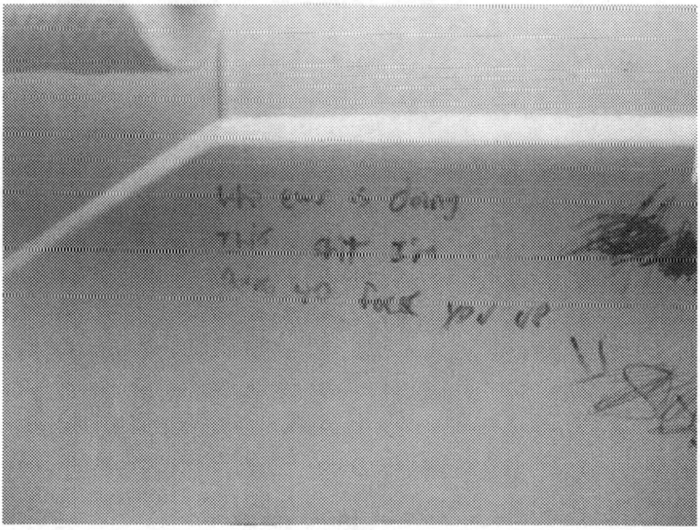
fuck you up

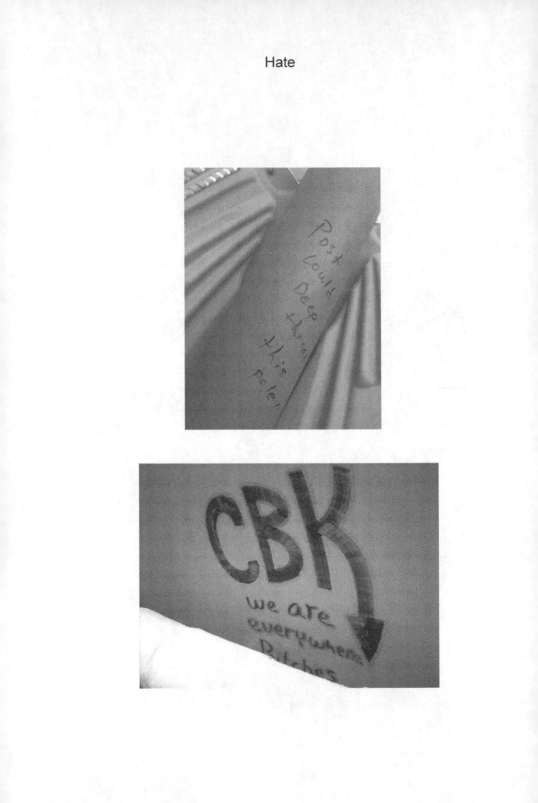

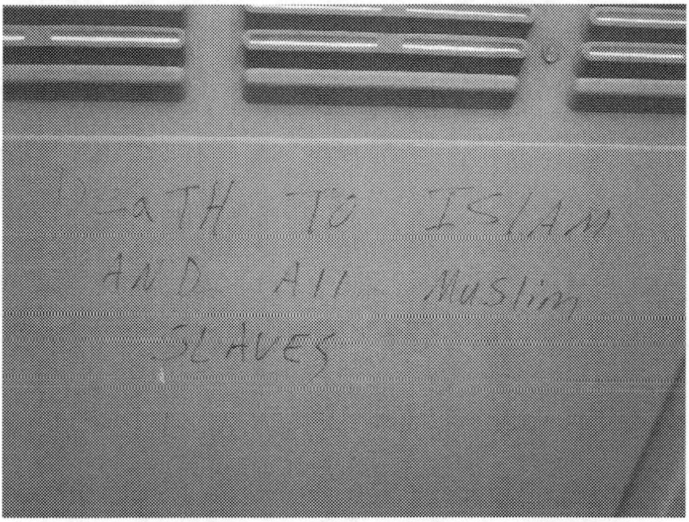
DEATH TO ISLAM
AND ALL Muslim
SLAVES

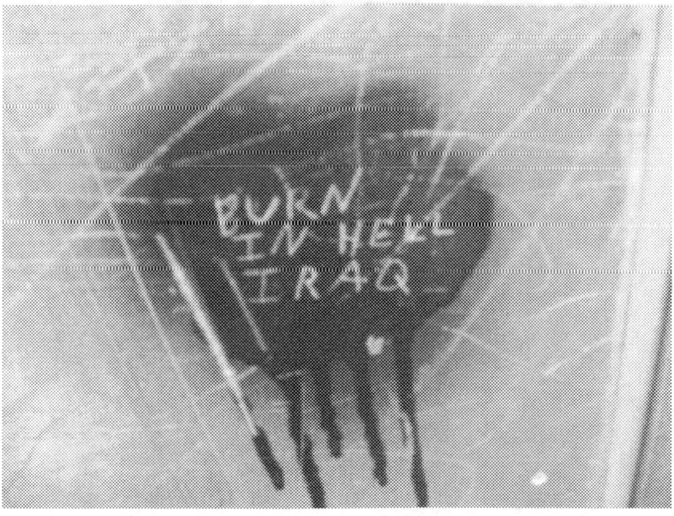
BURN
IN HELL
IRAQ

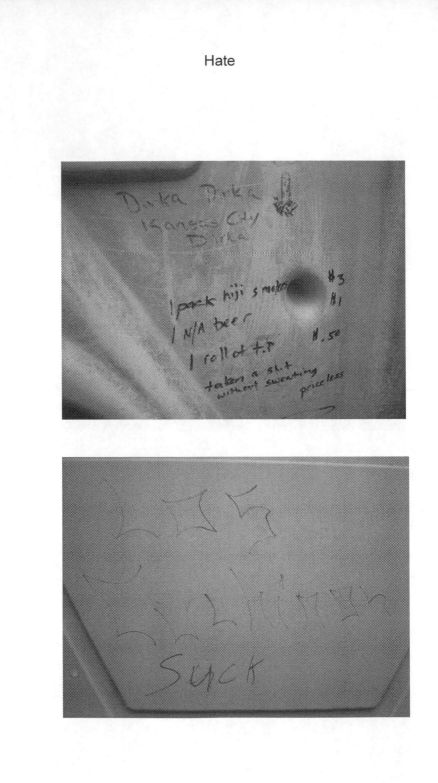

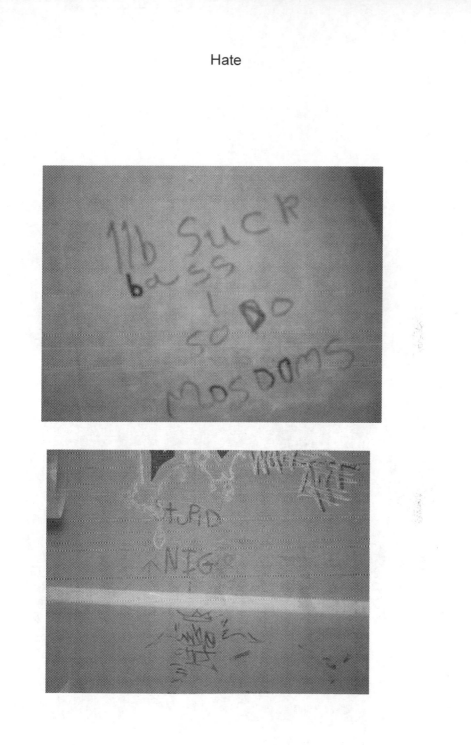

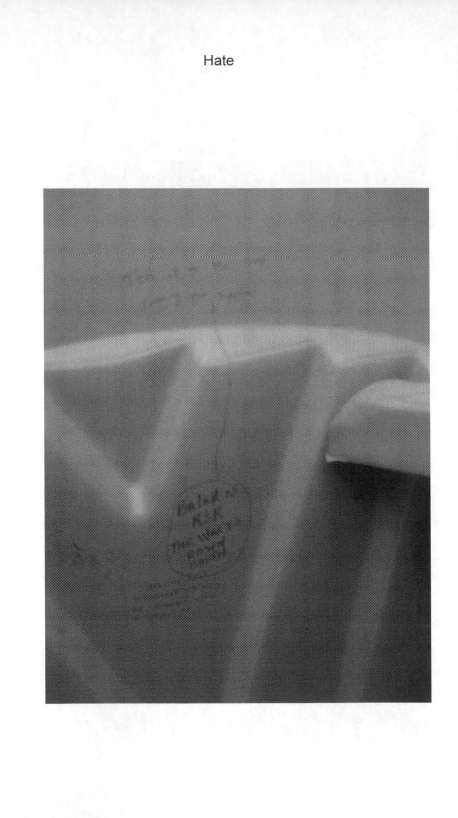

Hate

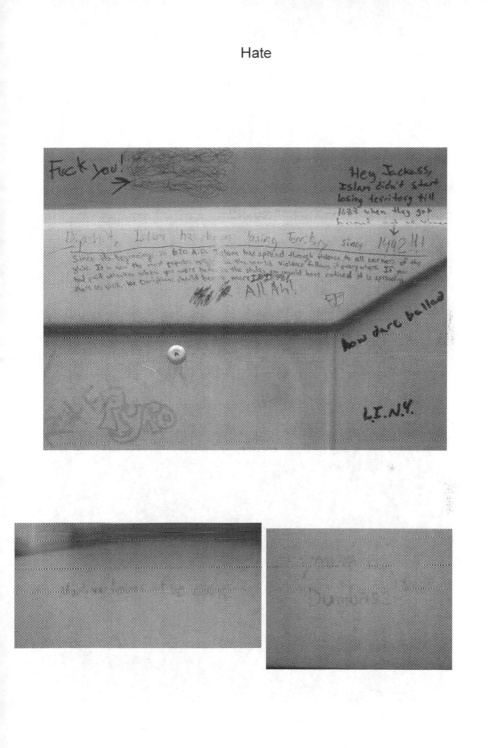

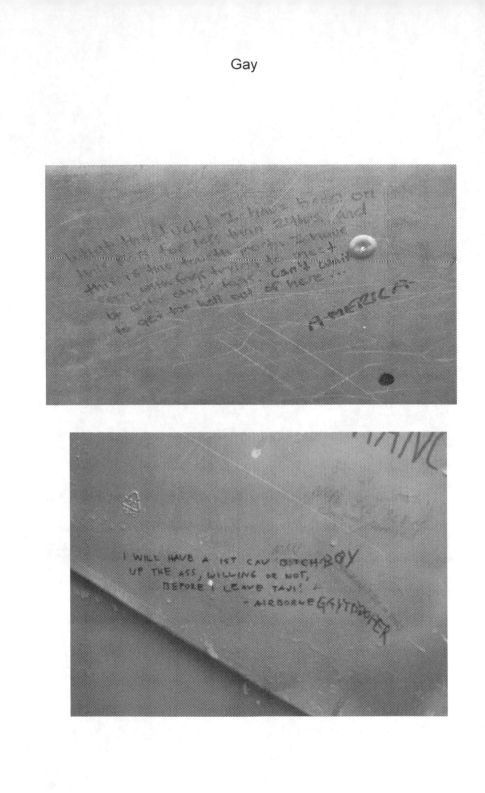

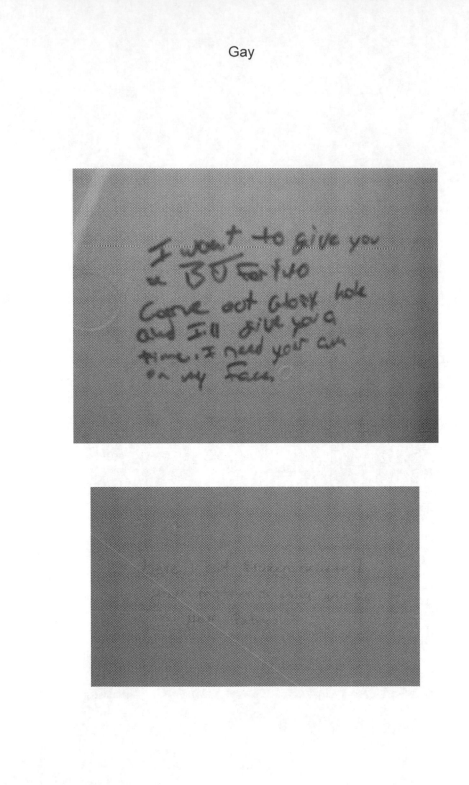

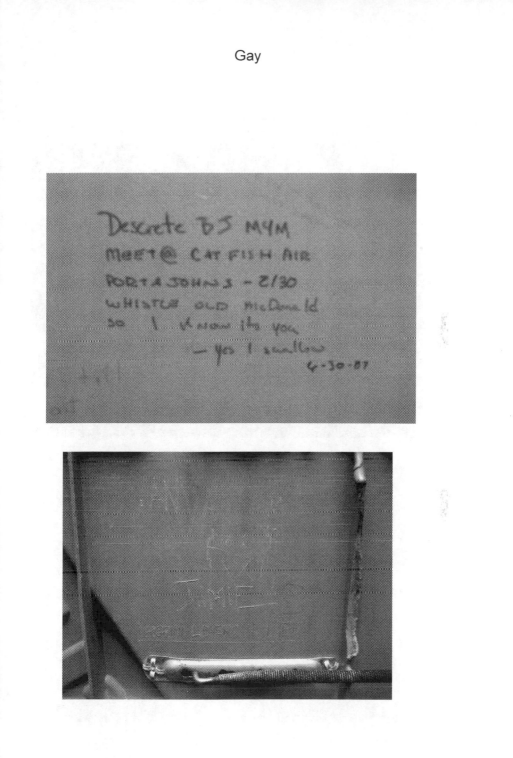

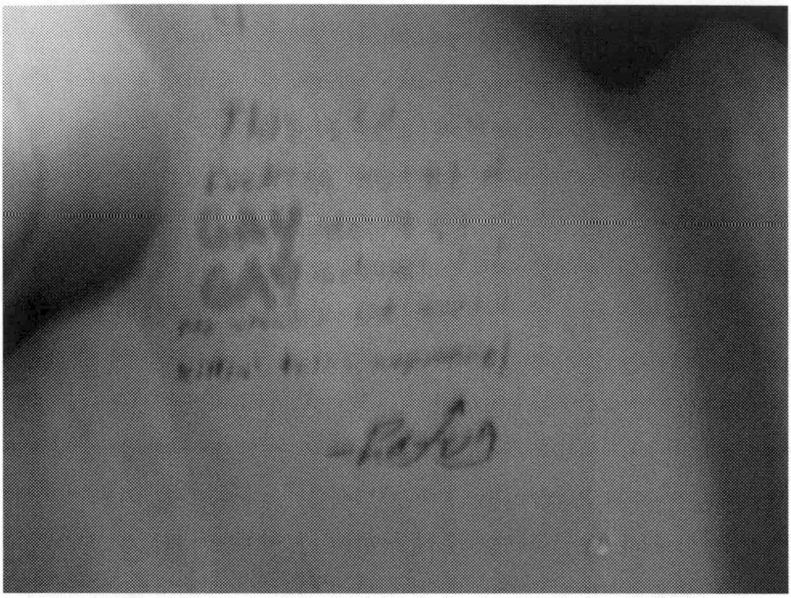

THOUGHT I'D FART
TURNED OF PELLETS
NOW YOU FAGS
CAN FUCKIN
SMELL IT.

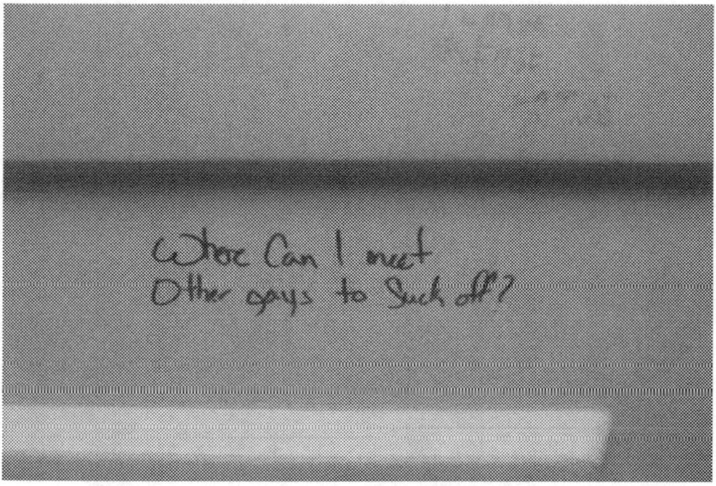
Where Can I meet
Other gays to Suck off?

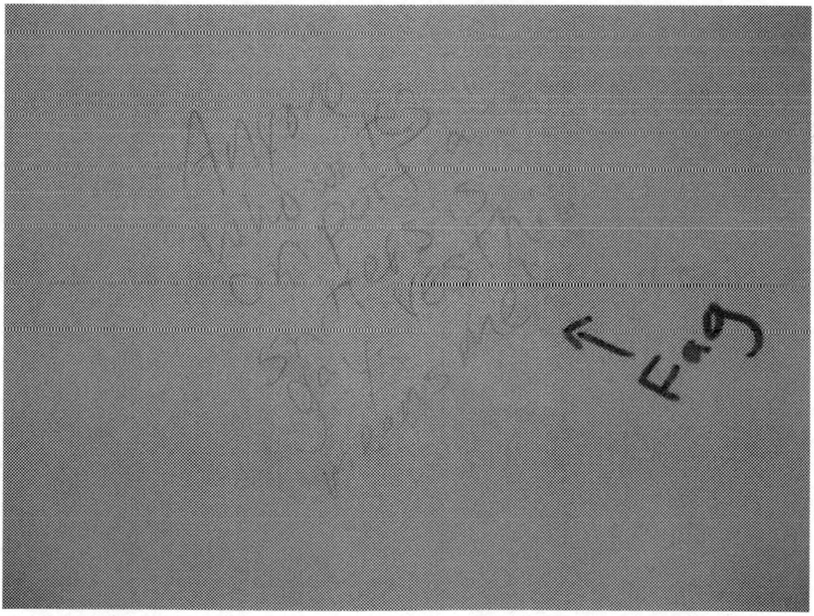
← Fag

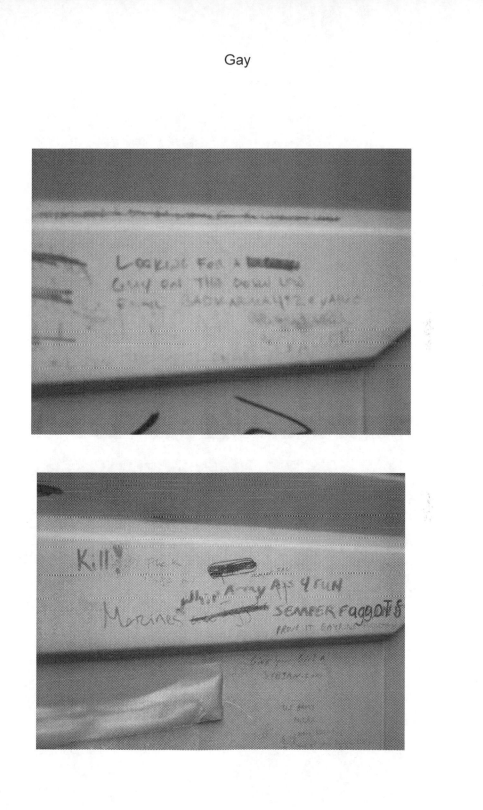

Gay

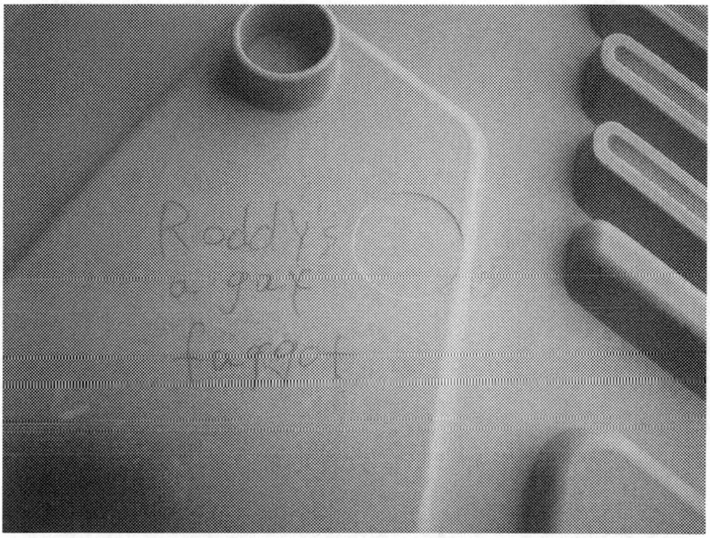

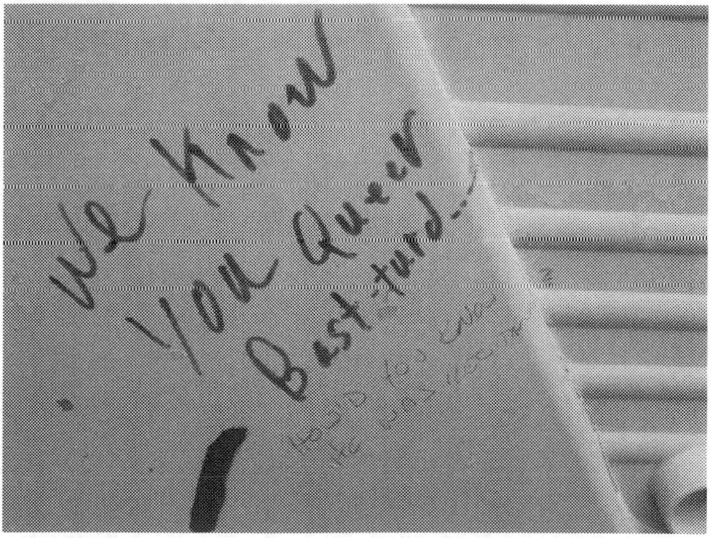

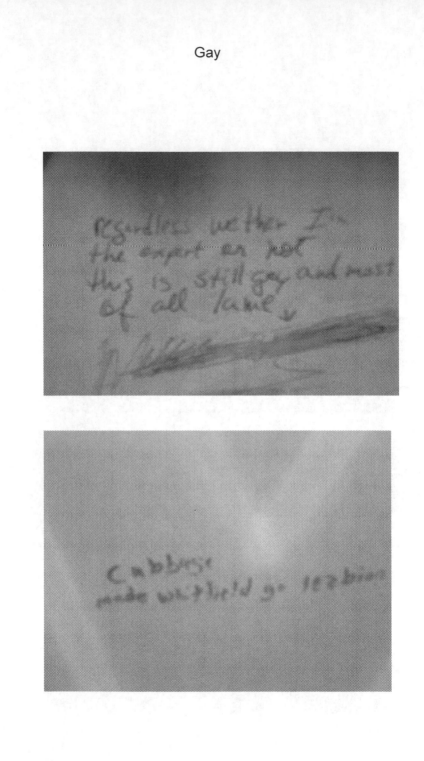

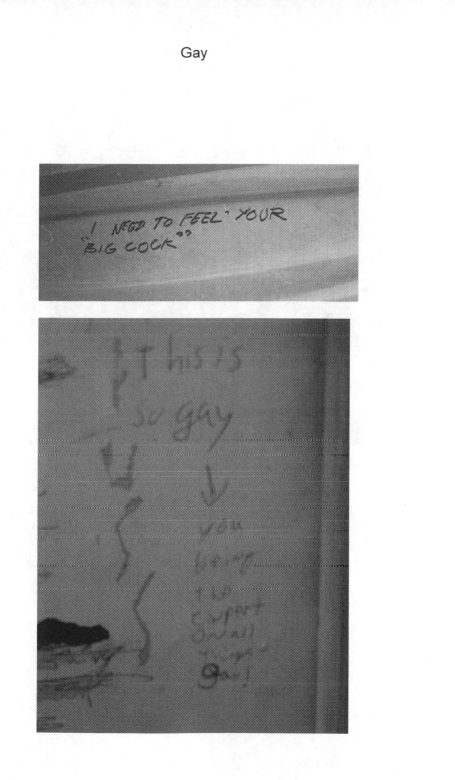

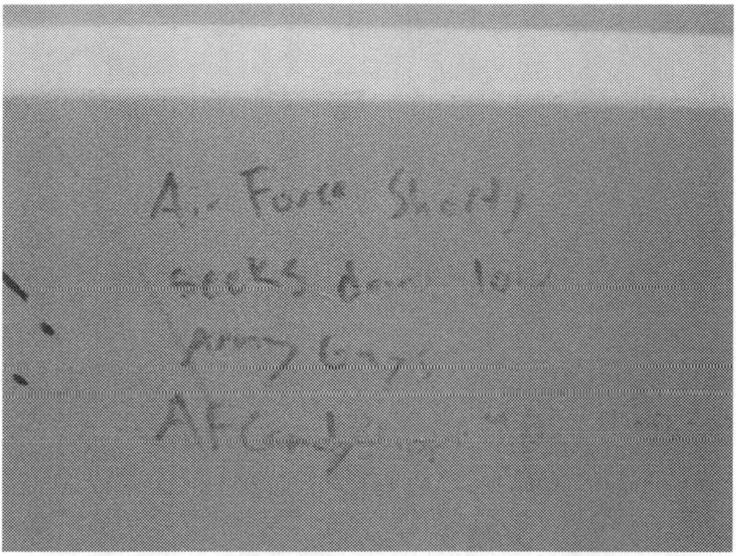

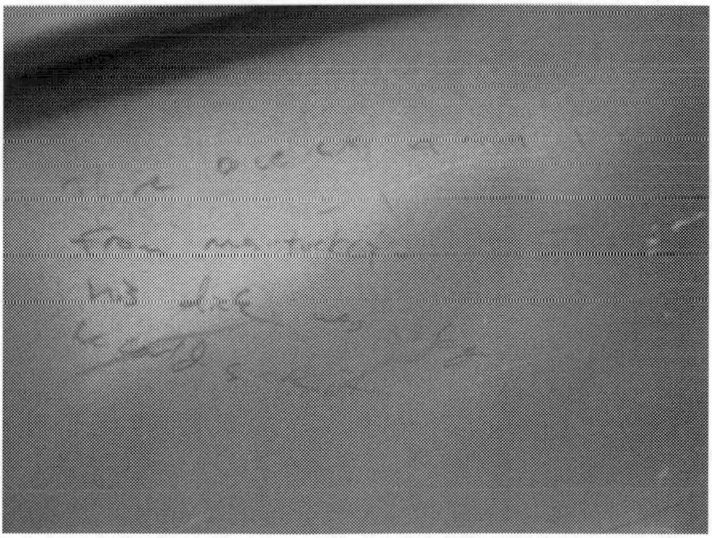

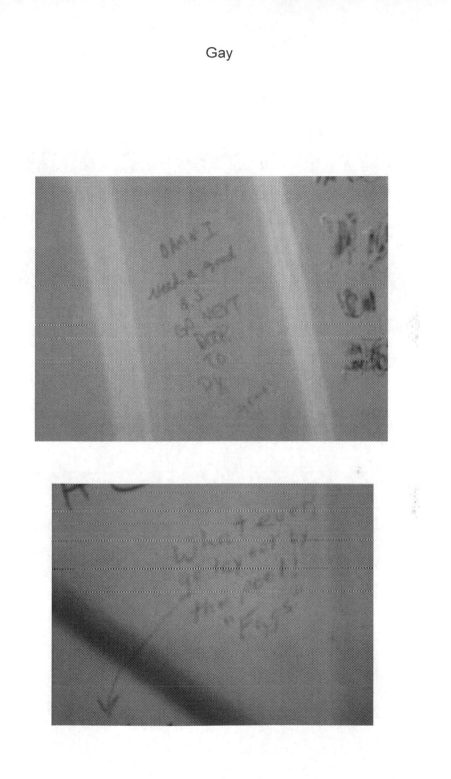

Gay

Is it Gay
to play putt putt
golf with a friend
And watch his little
Butt Butt when he
Tee's off.
And when a quarterback
Yells out hutt hutt and
he reaches down & grabs
his buddies butt butt.......
But wait I'm not done.
What if quite by accident
His teeny tiny little weenie
just slipped In.
Is that gay?

Supervisor Detestation

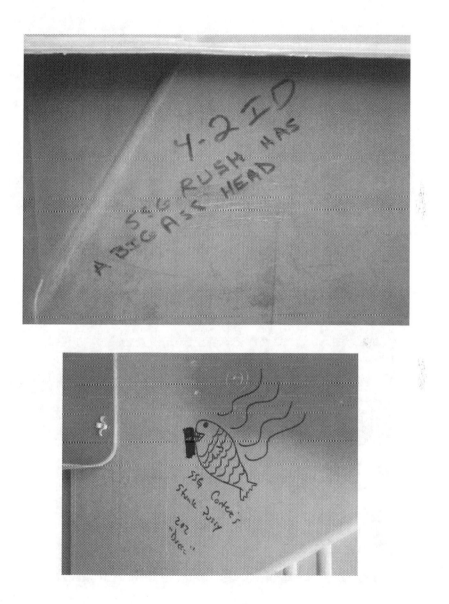

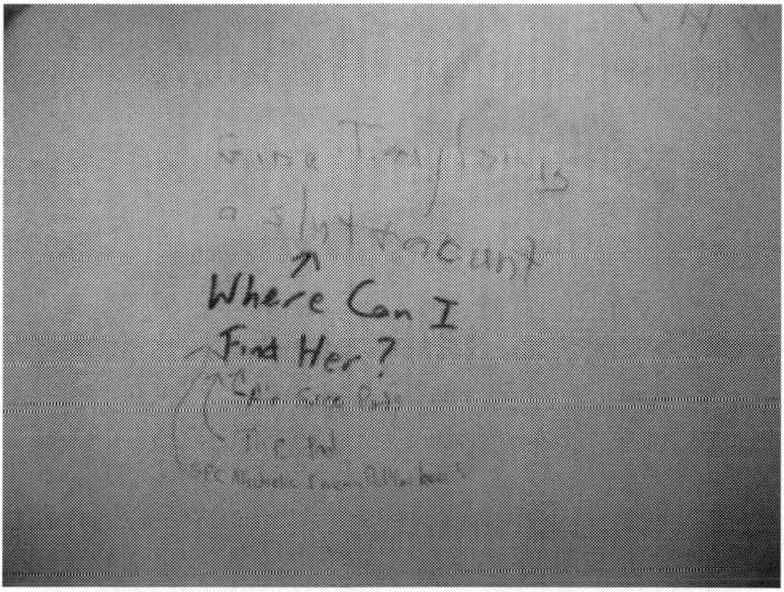
Where Can I
Find Her?

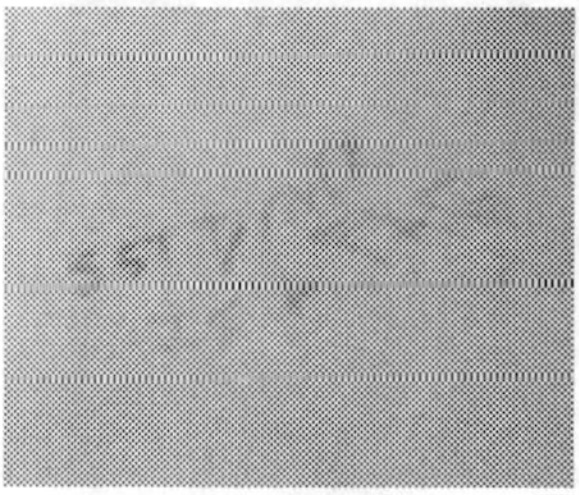

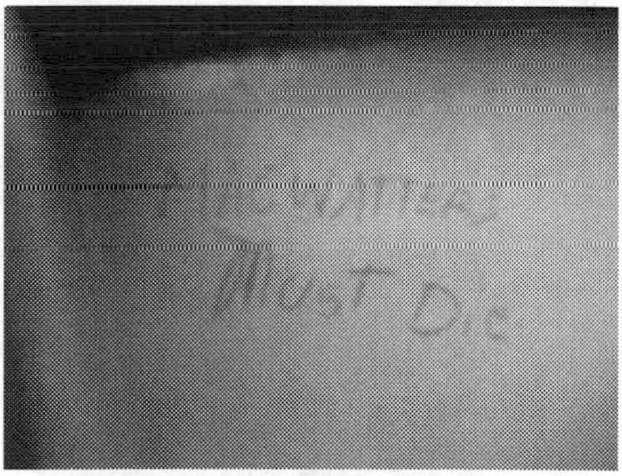
MUST Die

Supervisor Detestation

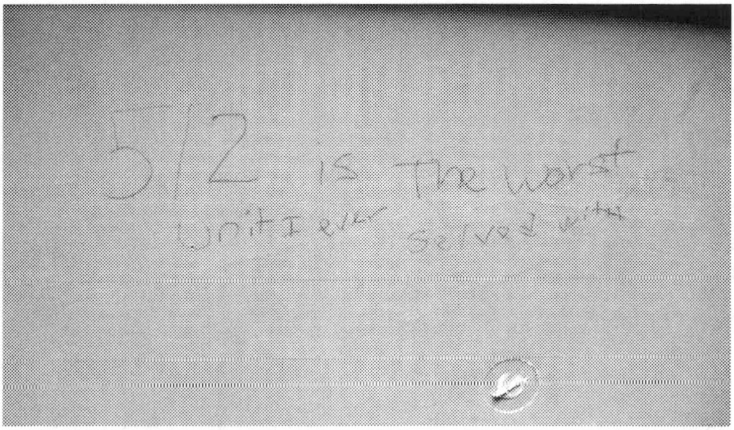

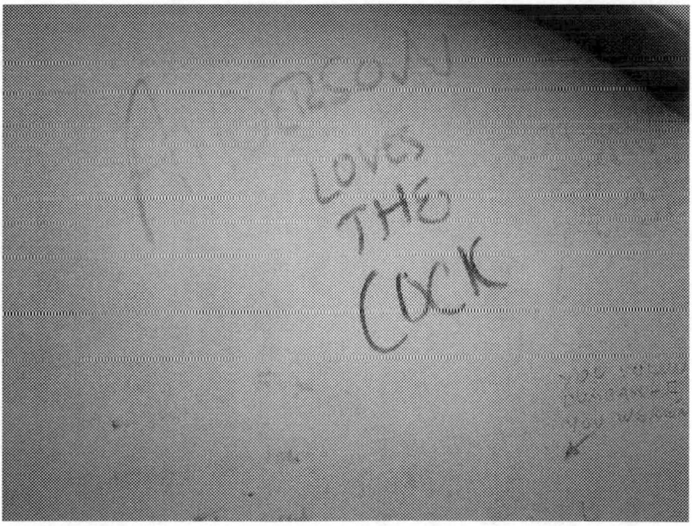

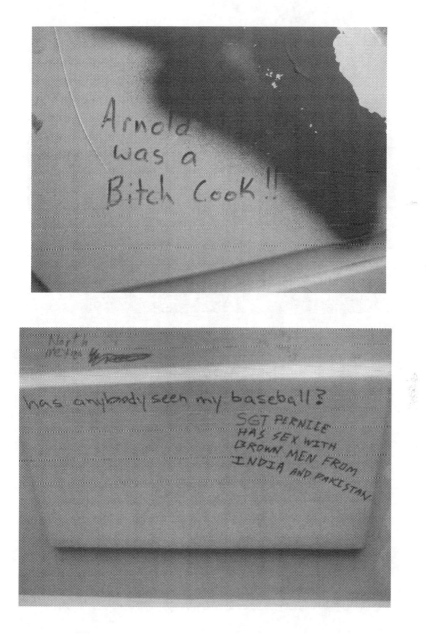

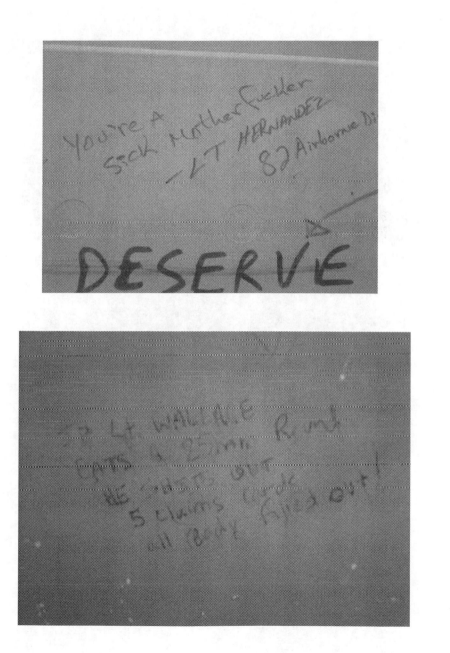

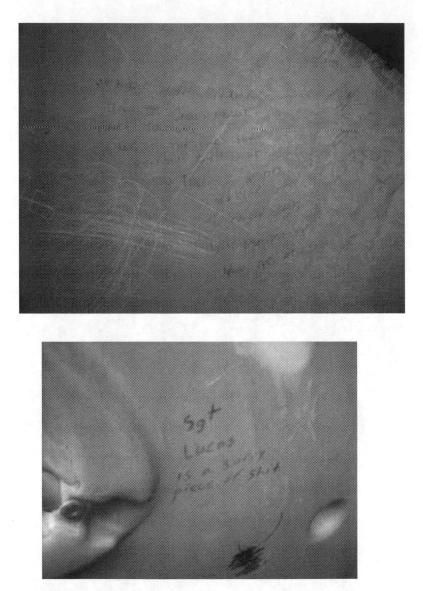

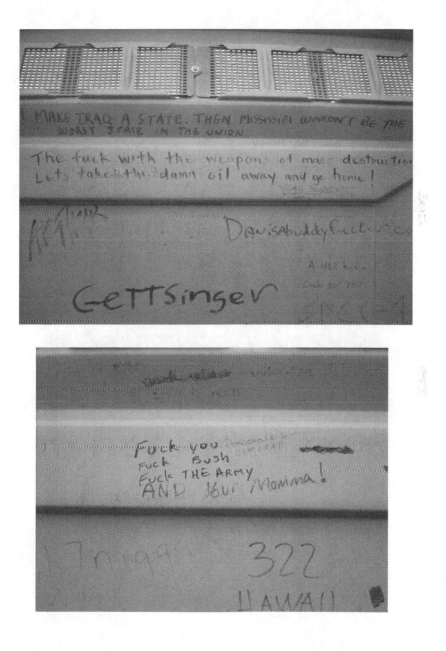

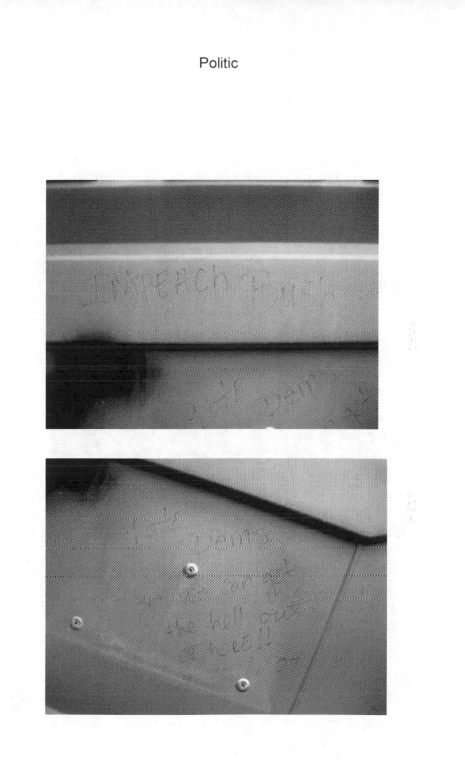

Q: Did you clene
YOUR WEAPON?
A: Why would we need
WEAPONS, we live at
Little Garrison USA
ANACONDA!!
YOU GOT SERVED
BITCHES

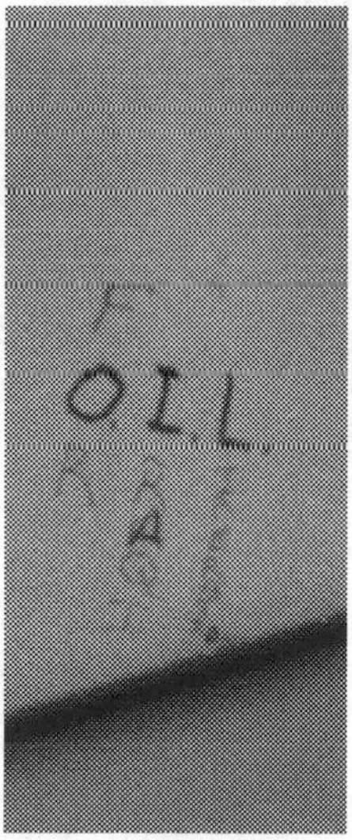
OIL

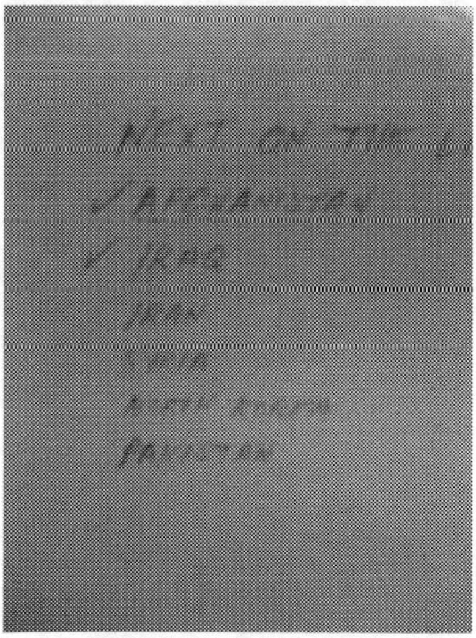
NEXT ON THE
AFGHANISTAN
IRAQ
IRAN
NORTH KOREA
PAKISTAN

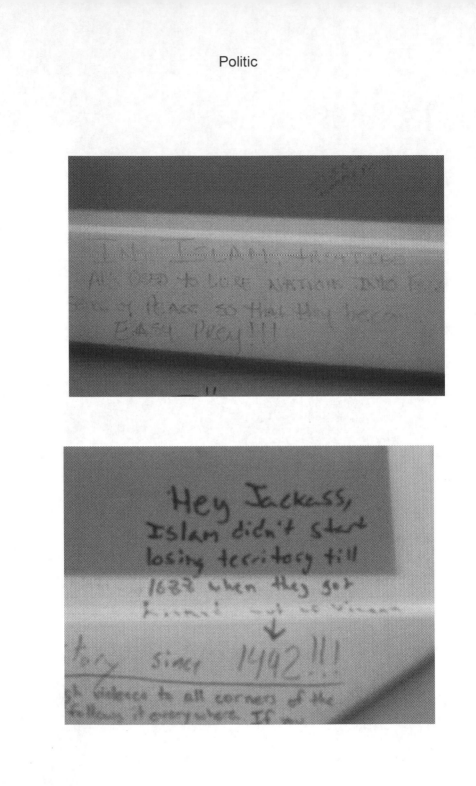

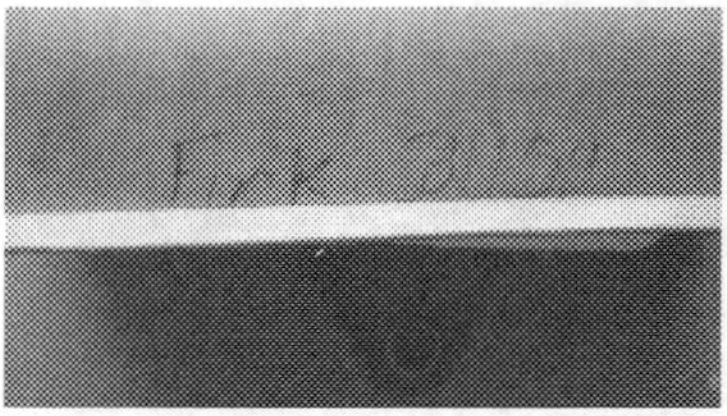

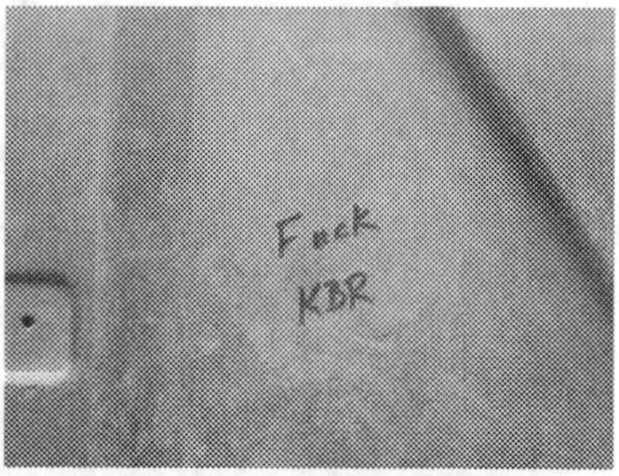
Fuck
KBR

PRESIDENT

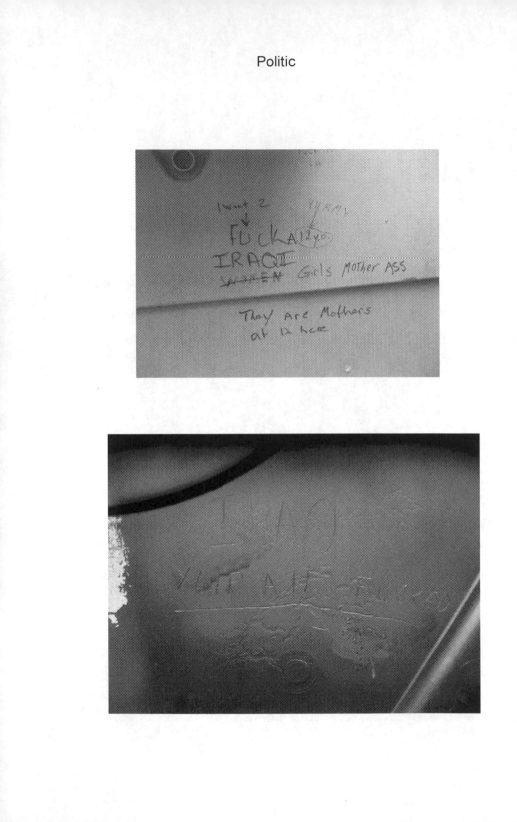

KBR:
$36 per plate @ DFAC
$35 per bag of laundry
Can't refill toilet paper daily!
Because it is priceless Bitch

THANX
Rumsfeld

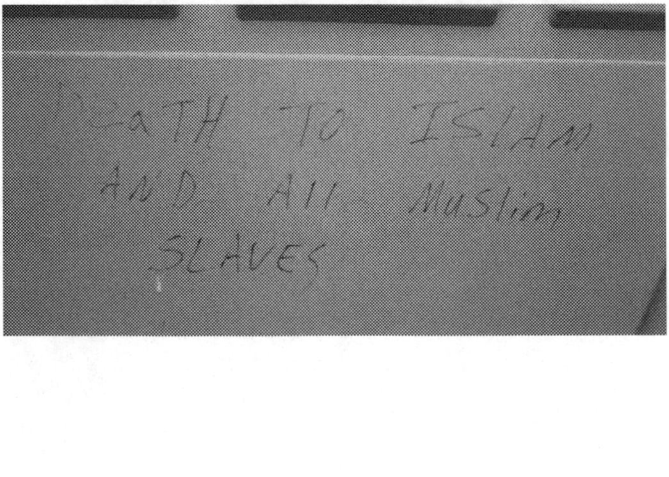

DEATH TO ISLAM
AND ALL Muslim
SLAVES

Politic

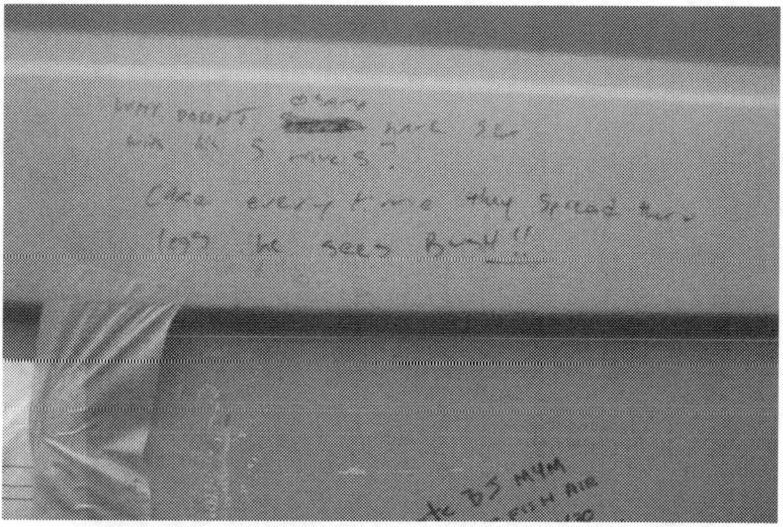

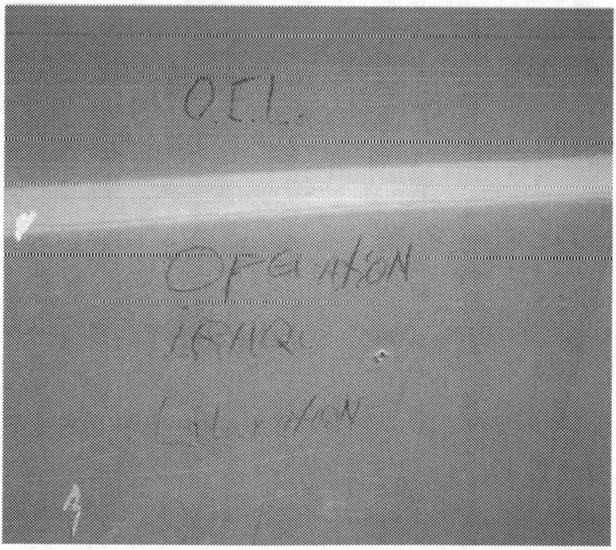

CHUCK NORRIS DOESN'T DODGE BULLETS, BULLETS DODGE CHUCK NORRIS

CHUCK Norris is SSG BABB'S sugar DADDY.

The boogey man hides in the closet because he is scared of Chuck Norris

Chuck Norris is gay

Kids have there mom o Dad look under the Bed for the Boogie man. The Boogie Man looks under his Bed 4 Chuck Noris

chuck is love

Chuck Norris Doesn't Mow
his lawn he dares it to Grow
Fuck
Chuck

Chuck
Norris
is
Watching
You!

Chuck Norris
doesn't have Aids
it to the people
he fucks

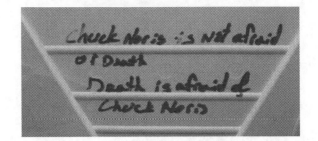

Chuck Norris is Not afraid
of Death
Death is afraid of
Chuck Norris

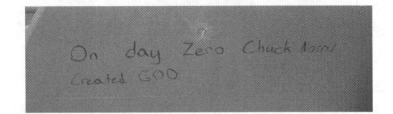

On day Zero Chuck Norris
Created GOD

IF YOU EVER ASK
CHUCK NORRIS "WHAT TIME
IS IT?" HE WILL ANSWER
"TWO SECONDS TILL" BY THE
TIME YOU ASK "TWO SECONDS
TILL WHAT?" HE ROUND HOUSE
KICKS YOU IN THE FACE!

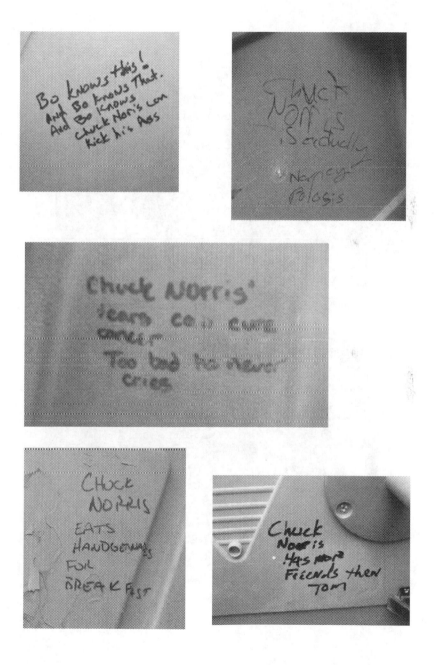

Chuck Norris

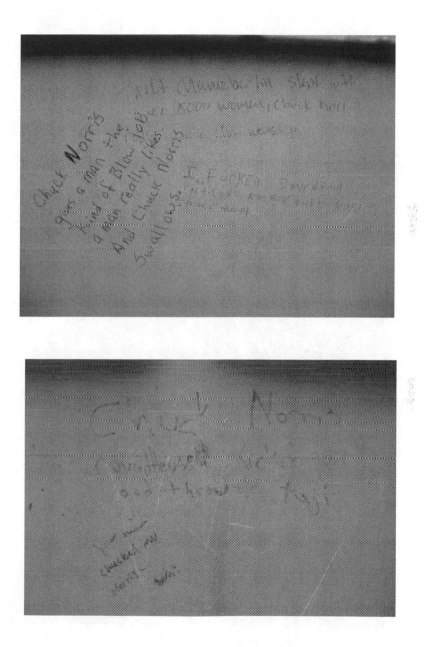

Chuck Norris

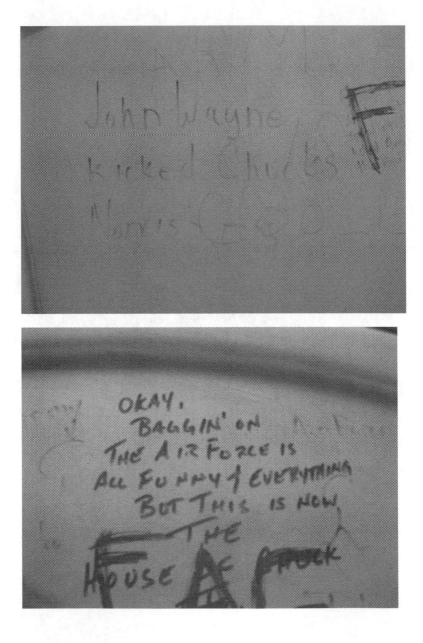

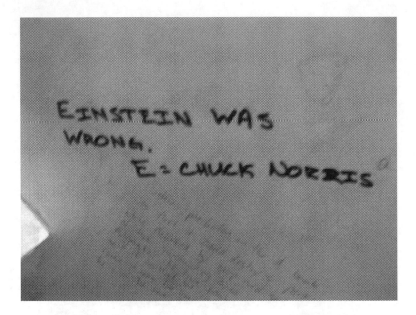

Chuck Norris

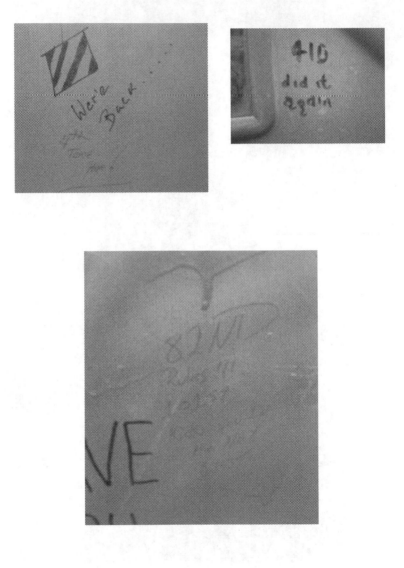

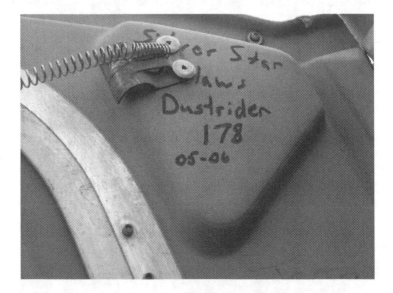

Unit Pride

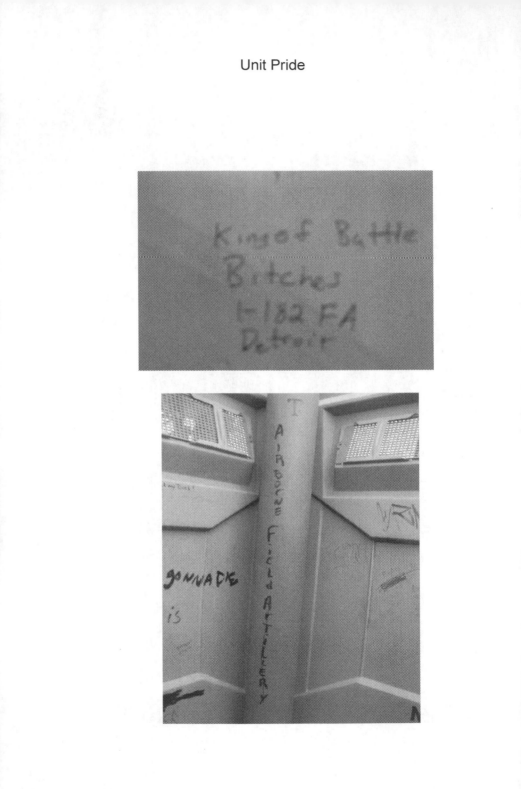

FT STEWART
GEORGIA
3rd ID
ROCK OF THE
MARNE!

TOO 2-8CAV BITCHES!
1-15 LEAD DA WAY!

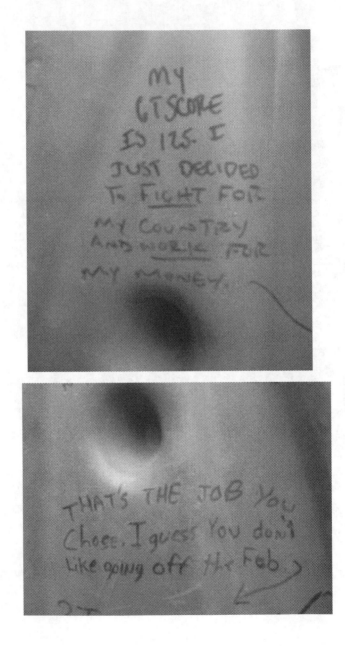

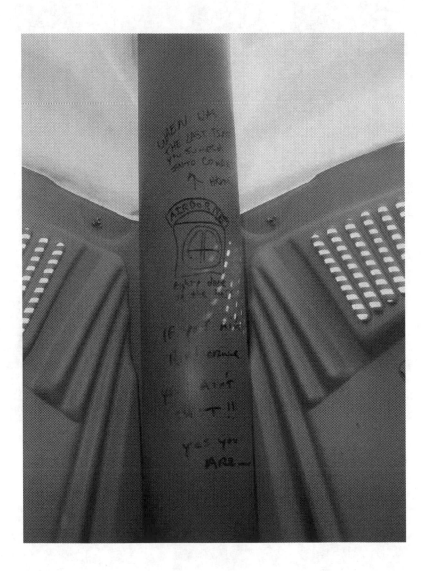

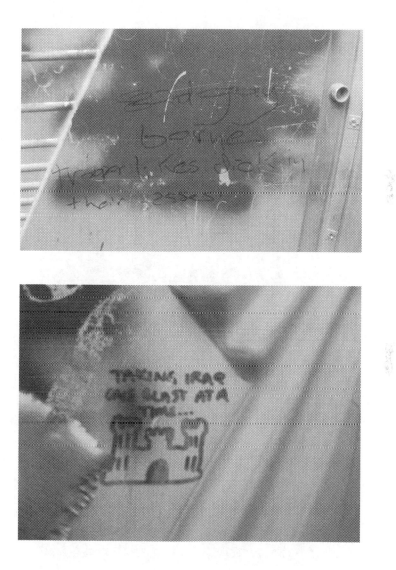

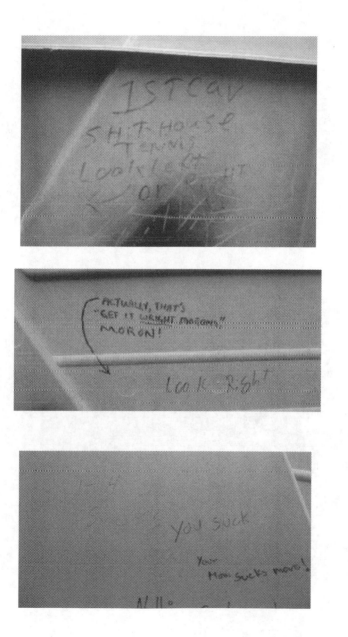

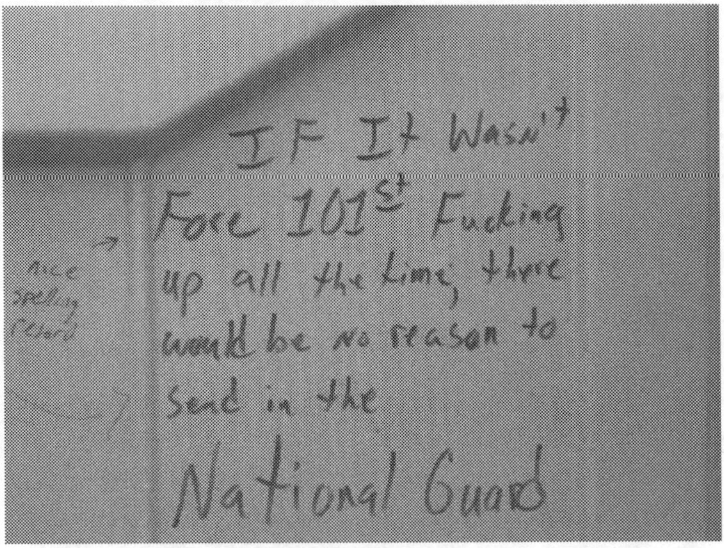
IF It Wasn't
Fore 101st Fucking
up all the time, there
would be no reason to
send in the
National Guard

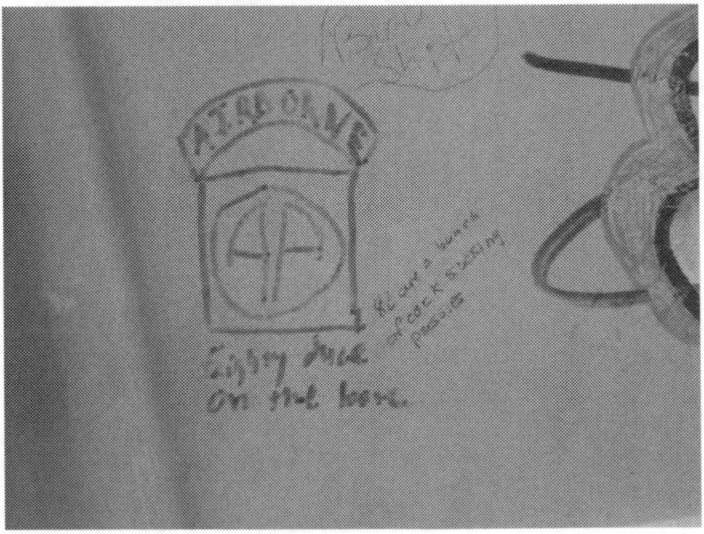
AIRBORNE
Eighty duce
on the bone.

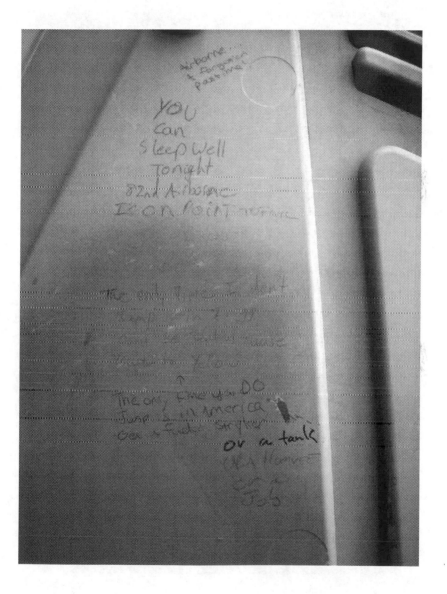

you are so fucking
stupid, you think
Ohio is the south
but it's not you
Dumb fuck!
One state under
Michigan does not make
it "Down South"

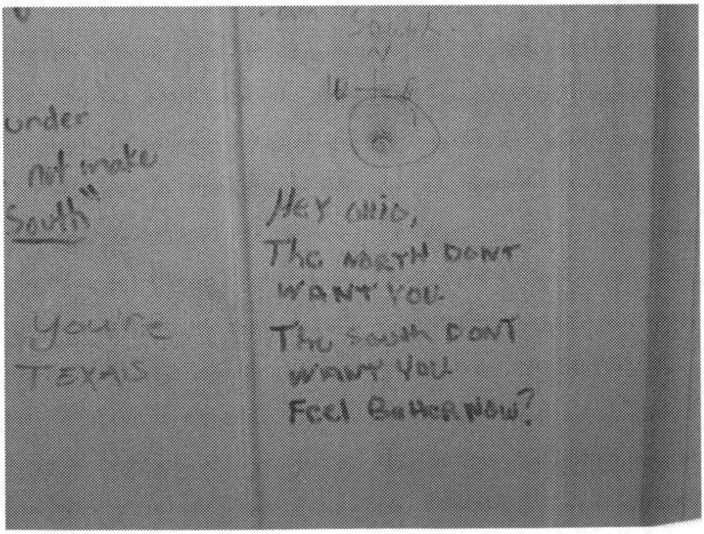
You're
TEXAS
HEY OHIO,
The NORTH DONT
WANT YOU
The South DONT
WANT YOU
Feel Better Now?

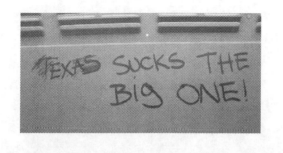

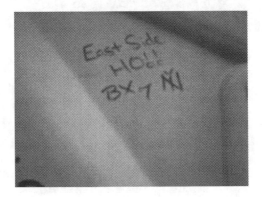

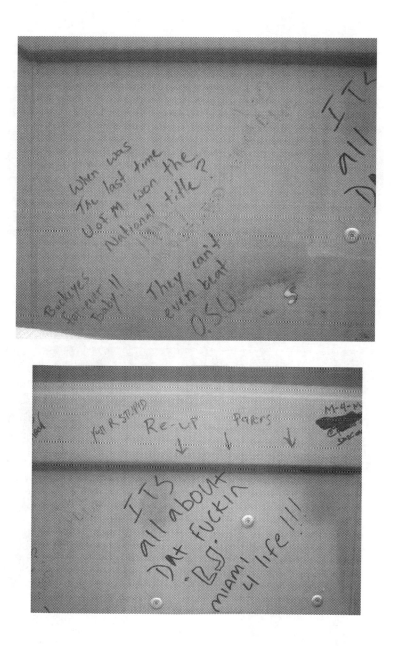

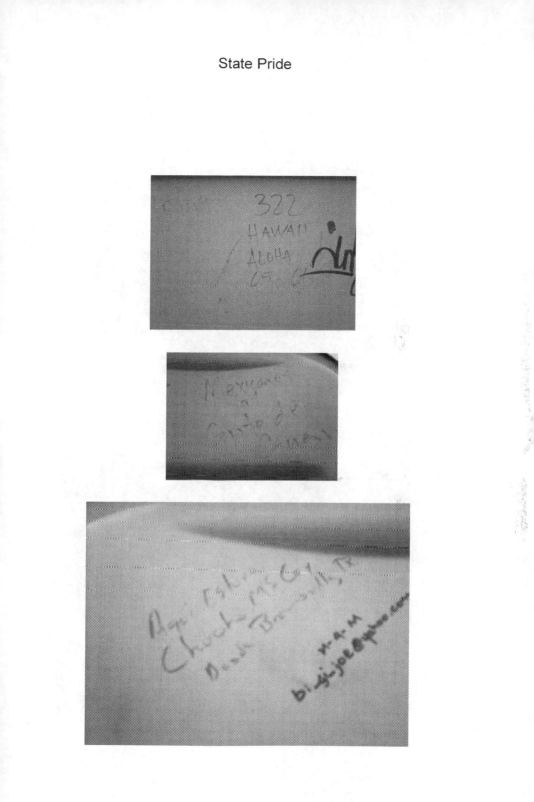

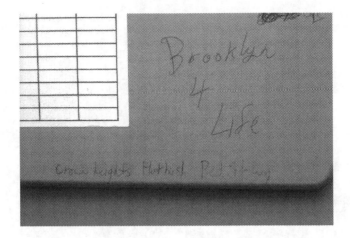

Contractors

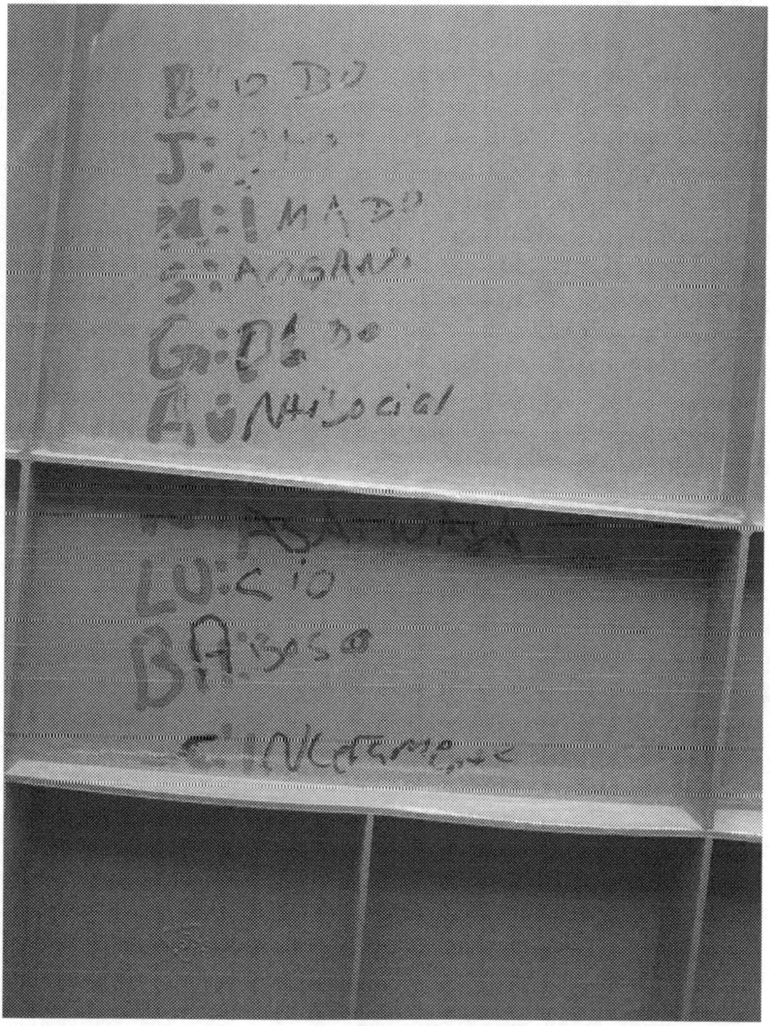

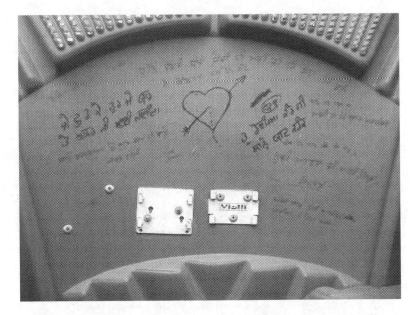

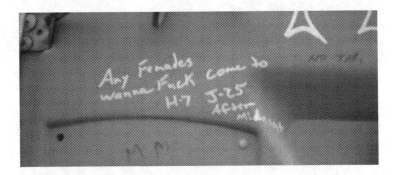

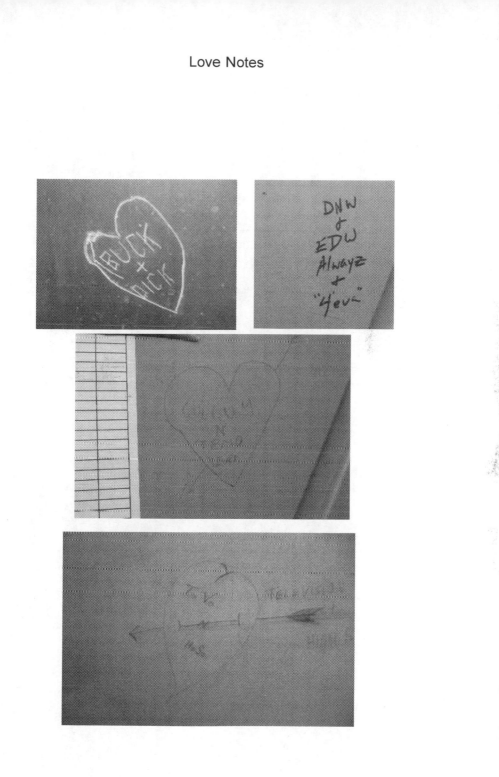

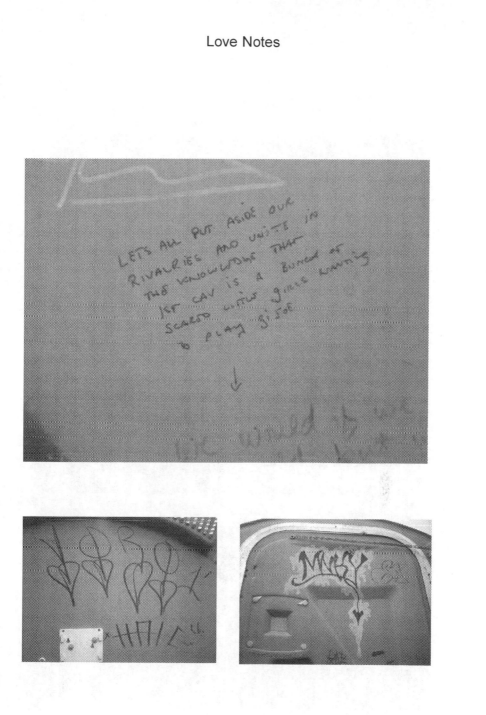

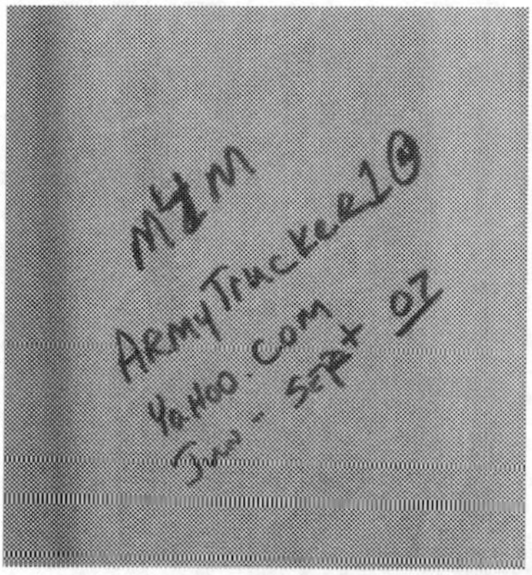
ArmyTrucker1@
Yahoo.com
Sept 07

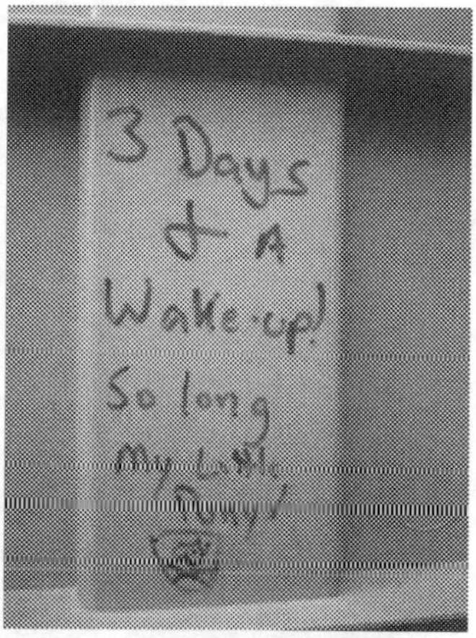
3 Days
& A
Wake-up!
So long
My Little Pony!

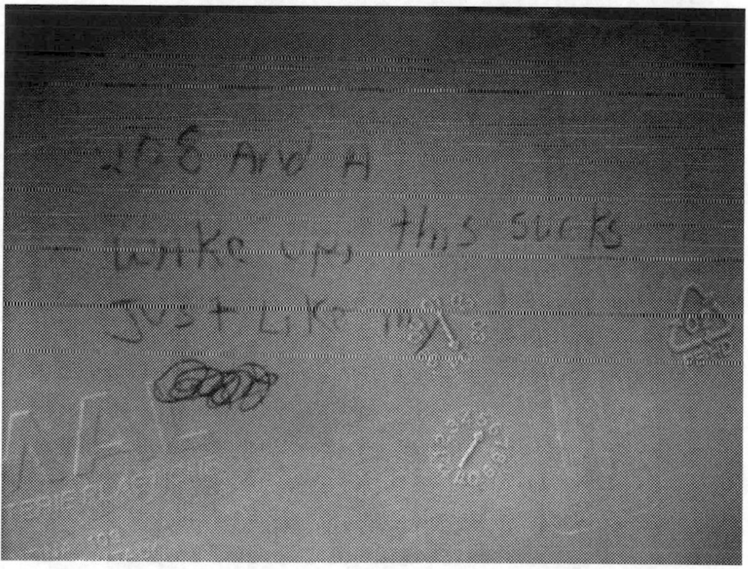
And A
Wake up, this sucks
Just Like my

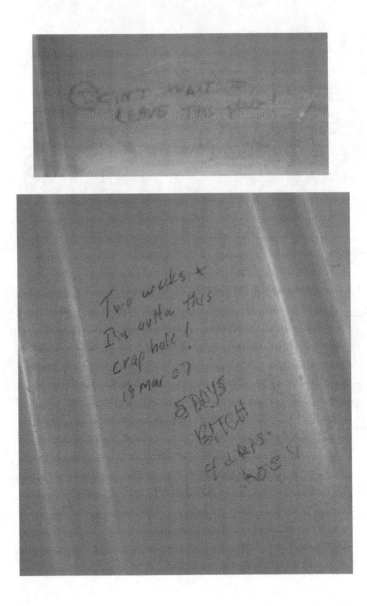

Count Down

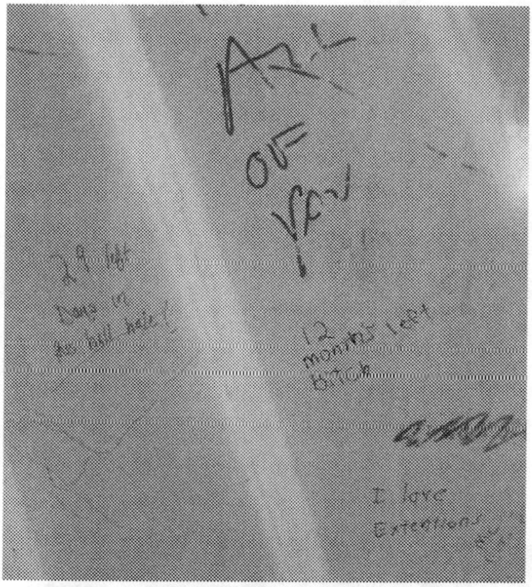
12 months left bitch
I love Extentions

8 Days Left

15 Months in Iraq Sucks
06-08
15 months in Balad is Like beins home!

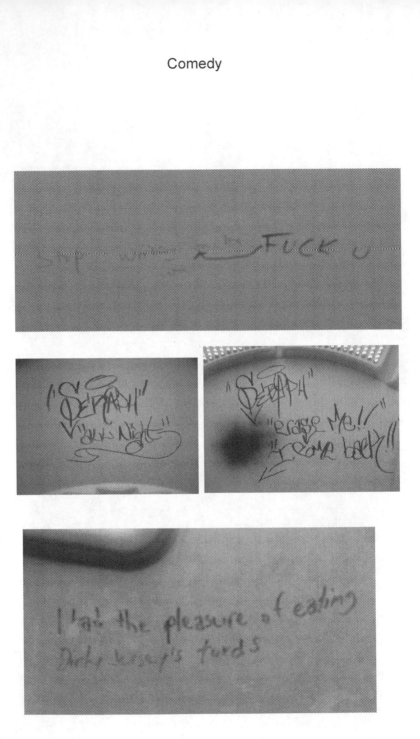

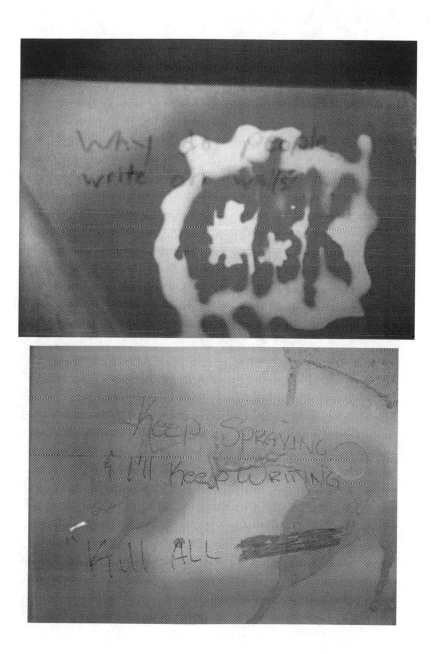

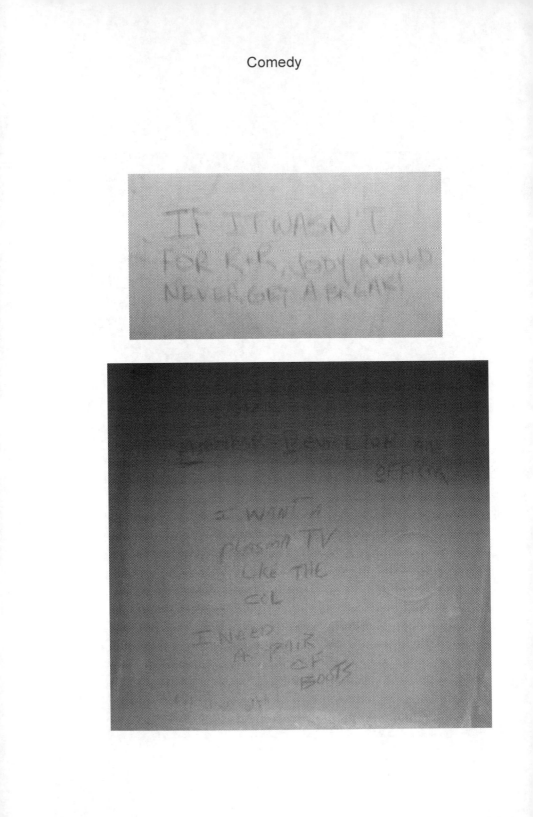

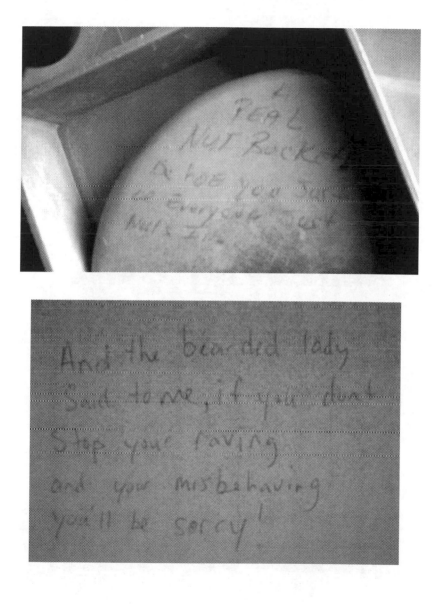

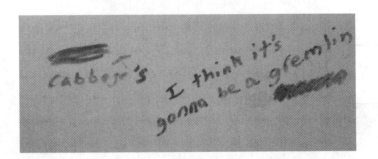

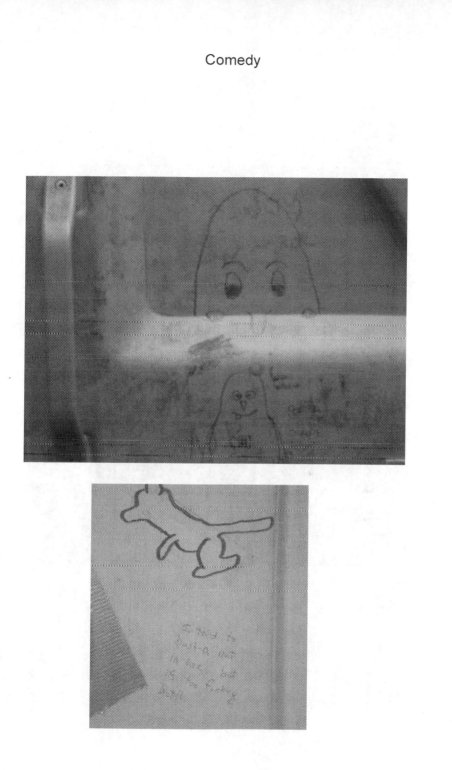

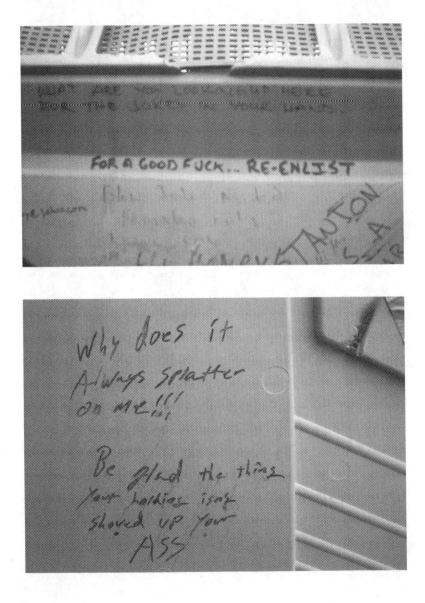

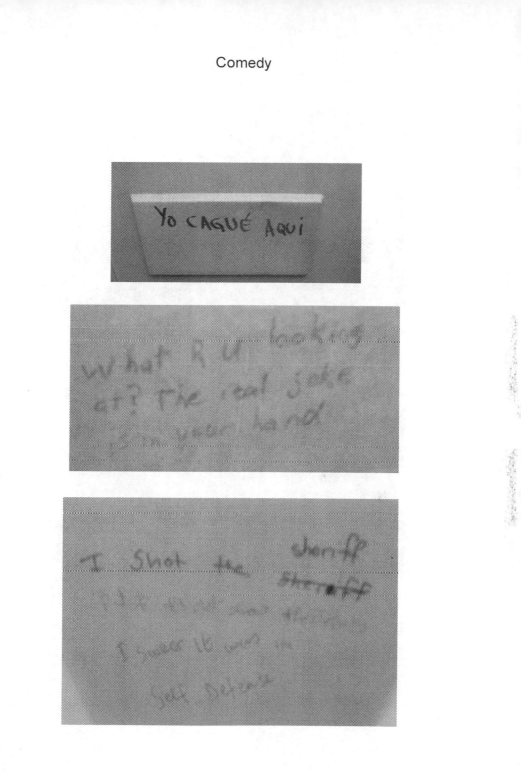

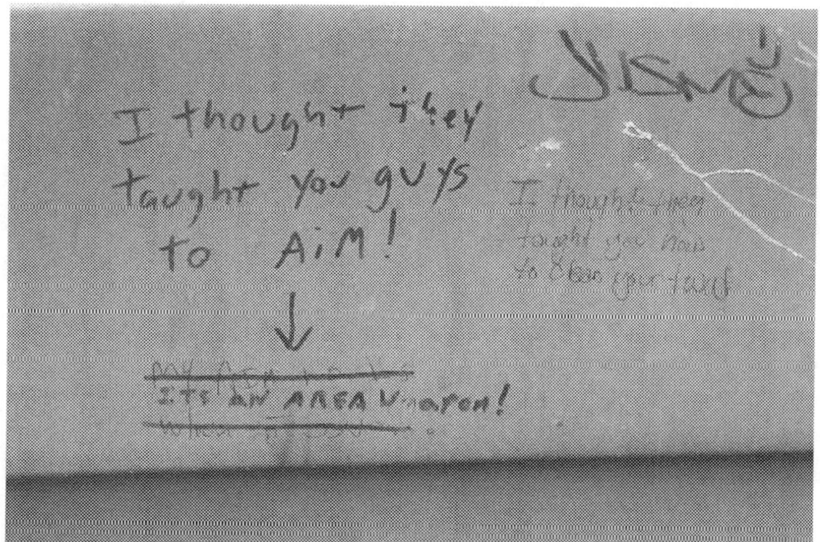
I thought they
taught you guys
to AiM!

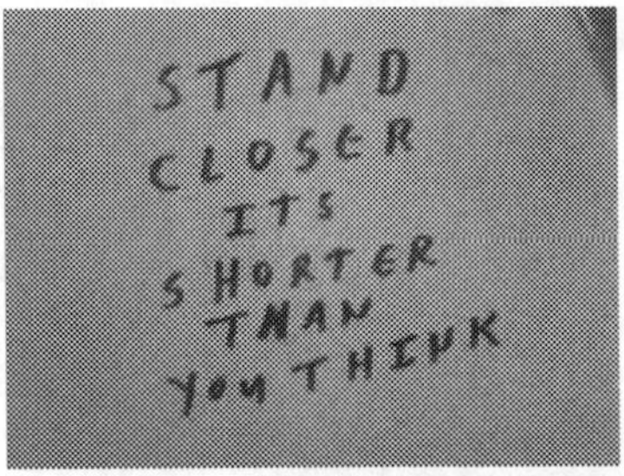
STAND
CLOSER
ITS
SHORTER
THAN
YOU THINK

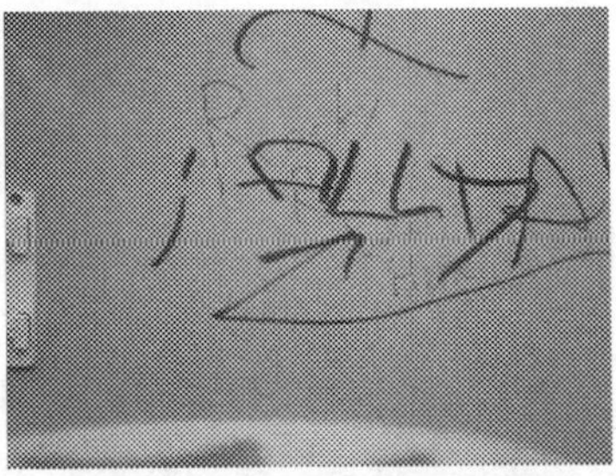

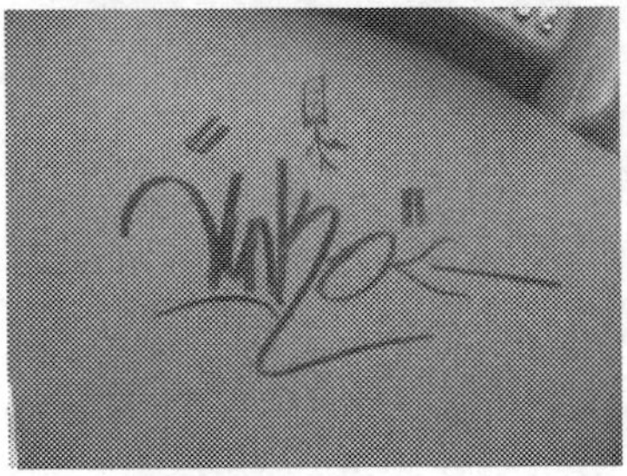

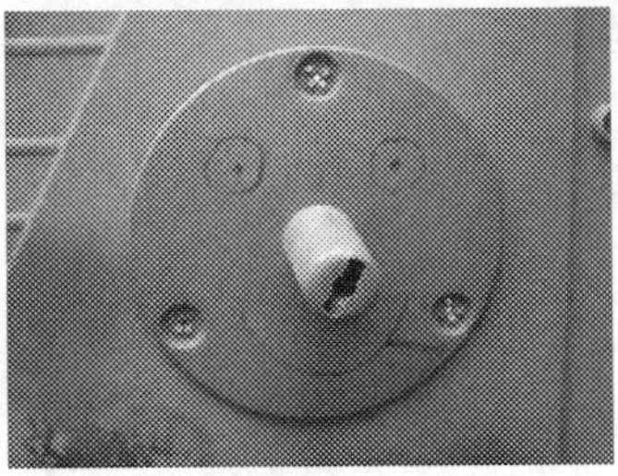

I can't
Read this

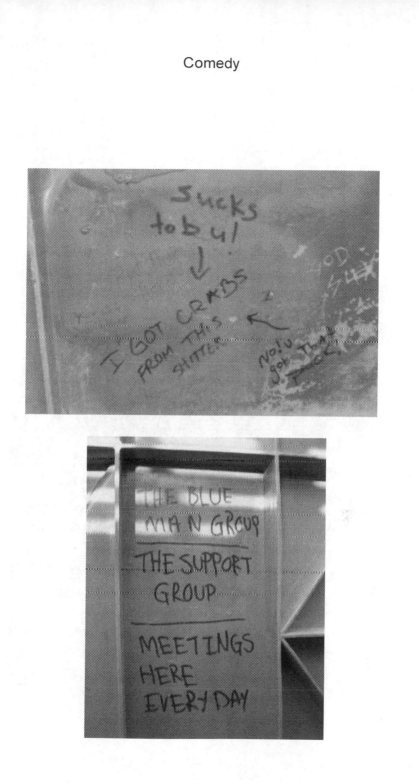

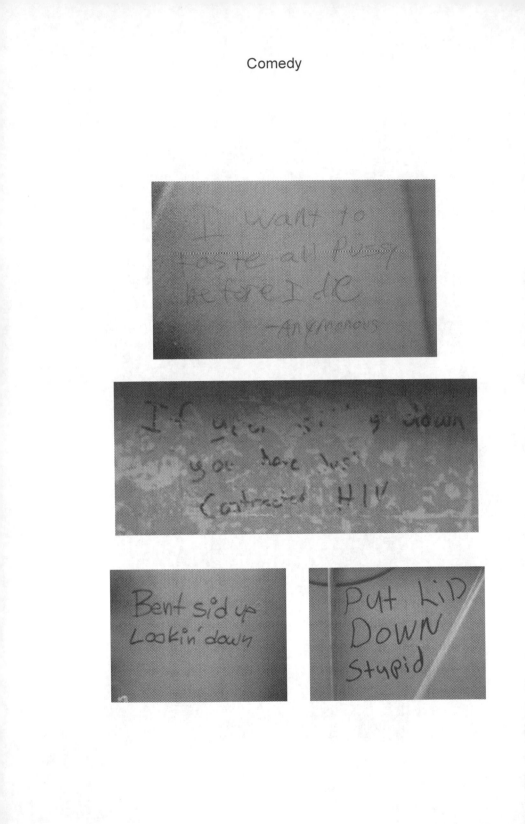

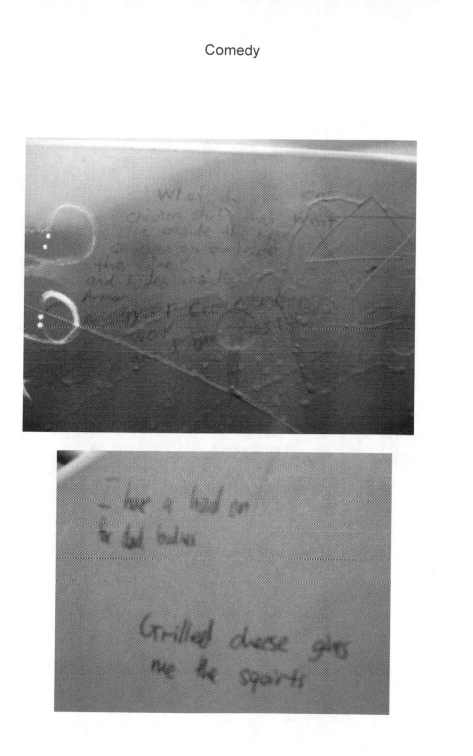

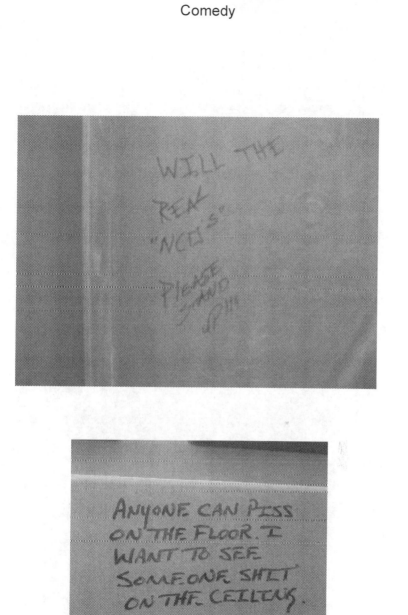

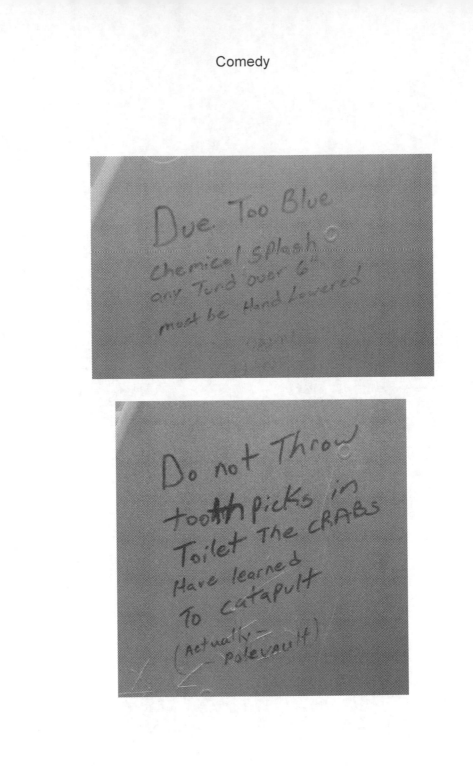

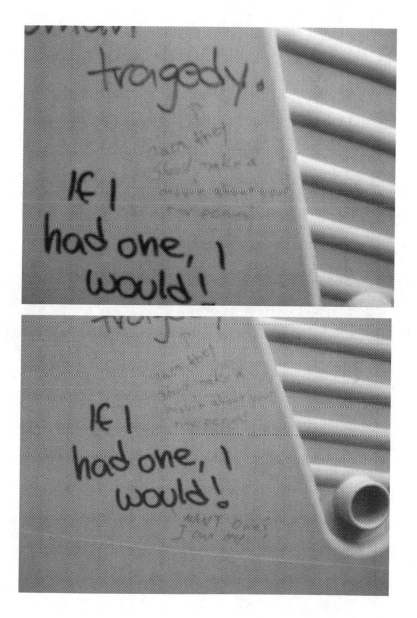

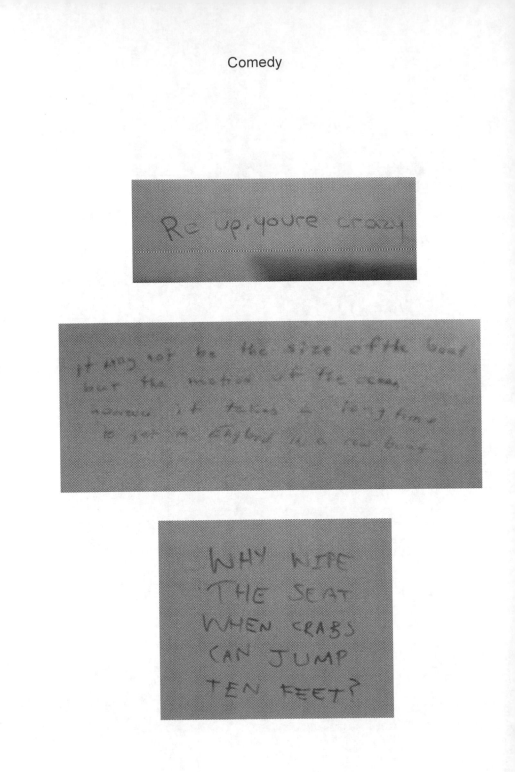

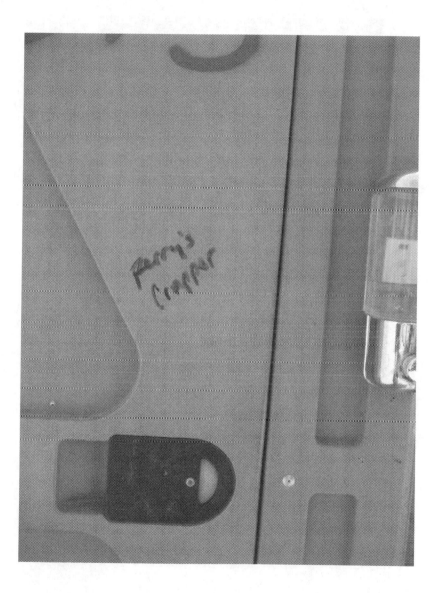

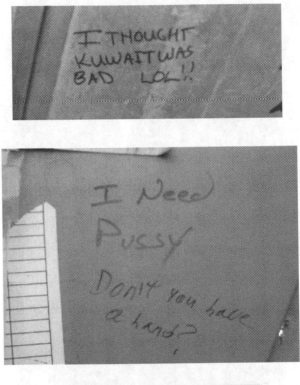

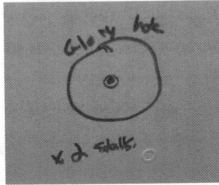

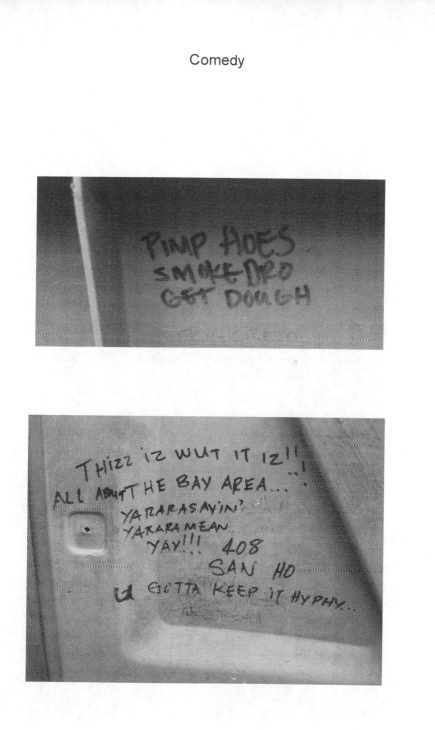

If this
is a Female
shit house
Why the Urinal?
DUH!
FOR CHICKS
WITH DICKS!

I don't
get it...
MAKE
ME!
It's 42, actually

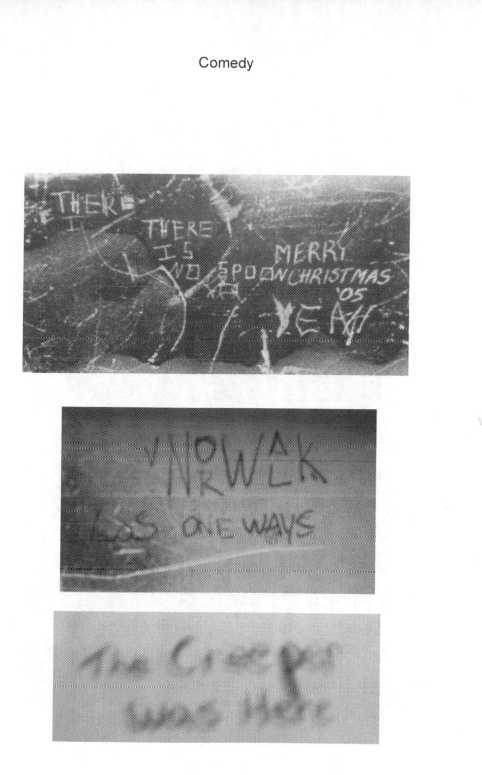

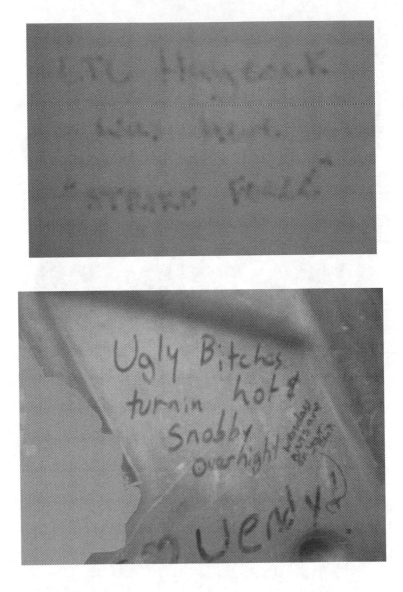

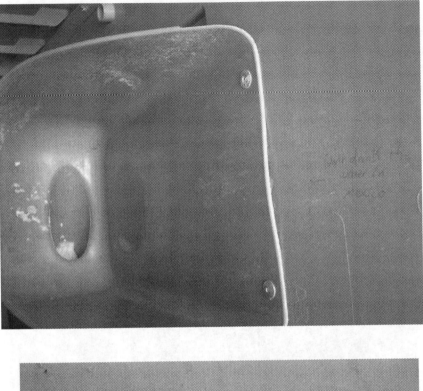

Glossary

The glossary lists acronyms with Army, multi-Service, or joint definitions and other selected terms.

Fobbit: A soldier or other person stationed at a FOB (forward Operating Base); a person who is reluctant or afraid to leave a military base.

ASVAB: Armed Forces Vocational Aptitude Test.

Re-up: To reenlist in the Army or other military service when your initial contract is up

FOB: Forward Operating Base

OIF: Operation Iraqi Freedom

BDE: Brigade

SPC: Specialist

SGT: Sergeant

SSG: Staff Sergeant

SFC: Sergeant First Class

NCO: Non-Commissioned Officer